DO YOU REMEMBER?

THE WHIMSICAL LETTERS OF

H. L. Mencken

AND

Philip Goodman

Do You Remember?

EDITED BY JACK SANDERS

MARYLAND HISTORICAL SOCIETY
BALTIMORE

Maryland Historical Society
201 West Monument Street
Baltimore, Maryland 21201

Founded 1844

First Edition

Manufactured in the United States of America

The letters on pages 25–182 are published by arrangement with the proprietors, the Enoch Pratt Free Library and Ruth Goodman Goetz, whose permission the editor and the publisher gratefully acknowledge.

BOOK DESIGN BY MARTHA FARLOW

LIBRARY OF CONGRESS CATALOGING-IN-PUBLICATION DATA

Mencken, H. L. (Henry Louis). 1880–1956.
   Do you remember? : the whimsical letters of H. L. Mencken and Philip
Goodman / edited by Jack Sanders.
       p.   cm.
   Includes bibliographical references (p.).
   ISBN 0-938420-54-2 (hardcover : alk. paper). — ISBN 0-938420-57-7 (ltd.
ed. : alk. paper)
   1. Mencken, H. L. (Henry Louis), 1880–1956—Correspondence. 2. Goodman,
Philip, 1885–1940—Correspondence. 3. Authors, American—20th century—
Correspondence. 4. Editors—United States—Correspondence. I. Goodman,
Philip, 1885–1940. II. Sanders, Jack 1943– . III. Title.
PS3525.E43Z482   1996
818'.5209—dc20
[B]   96-29348

For Lily and Sara.
All men have better wives than they deserve.

CONTENTS

PREFACE

July 2nd, 1919

Dear Goodman,

I have a complete file of your letters. There is a good book in the "Do You Remember?" series.

Mencken

THERE REPOSES, IN QUIET OBSCURITY, IN THE MENCKEN ROOM of the Enoch Pratt Free Library in Baltimore an extraordinary correspondence, never published except for a few selected letters. It is the most exuberant, whimsical, and nostalgic extended performance in H. L. Mencken's long letter-writing career. It displays as well the storytelling gifts of the affable Broadway producer Philip Goodman. These letters are the "Do You Remember?" correspondence.

It was far more than simple curiosity that brought me to the Mencken Room in the fall of 1992. I knew that I would find there the remnant of this great correspondence. In these letters I would see not only an interchange of ribald jest and heartfelt recollection, but the inspiration for the later books of remembrance both men composed. Having read and loved Mencken's *Happy Days* and Goodman's *Franklin Street*, I knew they were consummate storytellers: what they wrote would be worth my effort to find.

The "Do You Remember?" letters were intended as the starting point for what would have been a wonderfully witty book about the German and Jewish immigrants in America, but the book was never completed. As a first step toward the book, the correspondence that had kept Goodman and Mencken entertained for three years had been snipped into fragments. It was the wreck of a magnificent exchange, but I thought I had the foundation for repairing the stories and restoring to readability a touching part of American literary history.

I wanted to savor the essence of the book that was never completed. I would be the first person to read the "Do You Remember?" letters, in all their glory, since they were written in the years 1918 to 1920. But to read them I first would have to reconstitute them, and this would take a computer, a paste-pot, and a year of concentration. To understand them fully would require two more years of careful research. The book you now hold is the result of this effort.

The Mencken Room is a quiet and timeless place behind a thick, impressively solid door on the third floor of the Enoch Pratt Free Library. Access is granted only to scholars, so the room remains a sanctuary. I worked there for weeks, over a period of three years, and on fewer than a dozen occasions did I meet another soul in the room.

As I explored the Mencken Room, I eventually found the volume I was seeking—the thin, leather-bound book in which Mencken had saved one hundred sheets of typing paper containing fragments of letters. I knew the strange story of how such a neatly typed collection of fragments of letters came to exist. During those three years Goodman and Mencken wrote hundreds of letters to each other—some just short notes, and others extensive. Mencken did not save copies of the letters. But Goodman was saving both a carbon of what he wrote and the letters he received from Mencken. Goodman evidently had an intuition that something irreplaceable was being created in the course of this correspondence.

As the first step toward putting together a "Do You Remember?" book, Goodman, in 1919, handed his secretary both sides of the correspondence, and asked her to read through the letters, pick out the parts that cover his and Mencken's stories about early German-American times, and type them up. And so she did. In 1920 more letters had accumulated, and she typed them up as well.

Unfortunately, she did so in a manner that generated a haphazard result. She tackled Mencken's letters, but she did not start by arranging them in chronological order, and she did not type dates on the letter fragments. Then she followed the same routine with Goodman's letters. So the final product, the slim volume in the Mencken Room, has all of this wonderful material, but it is disorganized and undated.

When I looked at the first page of fragments, I found not only a joke inspired by World War I, but parts of three stories that had their beginnings and ends somewhere else in the correspondence. Where were the other parts? The same question has bedeviled every Mencken scholar who has happened upon these fragments in the past forty years. If I wanted to read the full correspondence, somehow it would have to be rearranged.

Here I made a key decision: I would reverse the history of the "Do You Remember?" letters. The letters had been moving toward a book of immigrant stories, a continuous narrative rather than separate letters. To this end the letters had been chopped up. The intended book would have been wonderful fun for Goodman and Mencken, but I simply could not write it. I decided to change direction and recreate the original letters. I reckoned that a book of letters would have a different focus, but would be just as interesting, as the planned book of finished stories.

Readers love an exchange of letters. Letters can be extremely personal, and may cover many diverse parts of the lives of the writers. These virtues are magnified in the "Do You Remember?" correspondence because the letters in fact do cover many things, including the business relationship of Goodman and Mencken, during which Goodman published two of Mencken's early books. I considered this a great plus.

What was happening in the daily lives of the writers found its way into these letters insistently and intimately. One thing we see is the pressure of World War I, a conflict that saw these men at odds with the lock-step patriotism of the country in 1918. Their brand of loyalty to their ethnic roots bordered on sedition; Mencken, particularly, was suffering for his German parentage and sympathies. Eventually the issue became conscription: if the war had lasted a little longer their jokes about being drafted and sent to war would have turned into grim reality.

These letters are a unique archive. Despite the fact that in a tumultuous century we have virtually forgotten him, Goodman was a superb letter writer. Some of Mencken's letters have been published before, but the usual book gives us only Mencken's side of the correspondence. Here, with the kind permission of Goodman's daughter, Ruth Goodman Goetz, we are privileged to see both sides. We see the narrative line bounce back and forth from one to another of the correspondents.

Goodman and Mencken write in very distinct voices, so that publishing the text as separate letters allows the careful reader to enjoy the difference. In these stories Goodman slyly reveals his love of incongruity. He shows us a happier view of the world. Mencken growls openly at the injustice he sees in the war years. Goodman loves human fallibility, and would not eradicate it even if he could. Mencken is happy with simple pleasures and simple virtues, but people can go too far in their loutish credulity; as they backslide into folly he rails and becomes sarcastic. They are human, all too human, Mencken thinks, along with Nietzsche. They are human (isn't it delicious!), Goodman writes back. In fact, Goodman would soon become famous producing Broadway plays that shone a gentle light on human folly.

To reconstitute the correspondence my challenge was to put the fragments into chronological order—to see what Mencken said, how Goodman responded, Mencken's reply to that, and so on. It is hard to laugh at the punch line if you do not know the line that sets up the joke. The first job was to find a way to resurrect the original order of the letters. One way immediately came to mind: why not go back to the originals that Goodman's secretary had used?

That, however, was not possible. Copies of Goodman's letters to Mencken no longer exist. We have better luck with regard to the letters Mencken sent to Goodman. At Goodman's death, Ruth Goetz told Mencken that she still had some of these letters, and Mencken asked to borrow them long enough for his secretary to type a copy. The surviving letters are currently in the Mencken Room, nestled right beside the slim volume of letter fragments.

Not all of Mencken's stories survive into the letters that Ruth Goetz loaned to Mencken—some of the letters had been lost—but where they did survive I reconstituted Mencken's letters to tell a more complete story. I restored comments about the publishing venture where they were needed to tell the story of the two books Goodman was publishing for Mencken and I made sure that the bitter jokes about the Great War survived.

Then I began finding the best arrangement of the letters. As I began the work of pasting together fragments, I used my computer to made a complete index of the names in the stories. The computer software effortlessly sorted the list into alphabetical order. This list allowed me to follow the stories through the more than three hundred distinctive names that appear in the letters.

Now it was time for scissors and paste. Having a rudimentary idea of how the letters would flow, I cut the pages apart, and marked each piece with the page of the manuscript upon which it originated. I began to arrange these new pages into order, to keep stories together. They began to form a chronological narrative. At this point I carefully read through the surviving letters from Mencken to Goodman. I was able to supply dates for some of Mencken's side of the correspondence, and this gave me a few more clues about which letters came first.

As I considered the text that was taking shape, I discovered that rearranging the correspondence into its original order was only half the job of bringing it back to life. A very great deal has changed during the years since World War I. I would have to supply through annotations the background for most of the stories that Mencken and Goodman were exchanging. I have become a devoted advocate of annotations. Letters from the past are great fun to read, but too often they are presented without explanation. This seems the waste of a great opportunity. It is like being dropped off in a fascinating neighborhood, with interesting homes on all sides, but no one has thought to introduce us to the inhabitants, and knowing not a soul, we wander on, oblivious to the marvelous lives on all sides.

It has been three years since I started to transform what was a jumble of correspondence back to its original humor, insight, and sparkle. You now hold the final product. I hope that your journey through the letters is as much fun as mine has been.

J.S.
San Diego
April 1996

DO YOU REMEMBER?

INTRODUCTION

At lunch, Goodman, a Gargantuan eater, had wolfed down a huge steak with all the trimmings, topped off with four or five of the sandwiches sold for a nickel each at the Hofbräu bar in lieu of free lunch. He not only had the enormous paunch but the bawdy wit of Falstaff. Both he and Mencken enjoyed good food, good drink, and a good story. For many years they corresponded constantly, spicing their letters with some of the most pungent Rabelaisian humor ever penned.—Sara Mayfield, *The Constant Circle* (1968)

H. L. MENCKEN IS STILL A SUBJECT OF CONTROVERSY, FORTY years after his death. Books of his observations, newspaper articles, or letters make news every year, most recently *A Second Mencken Chrestomathy* and *In Defense of Marion: The Love of Marion Bloom and H. L. Mencken,* by Edward A. Martin. As a result, the author of *The American Language* and editor of *The Smart Set* and *American Mercury* magazines does not need a long introduction here. For further reading, Professor Fred

Hobson's *Mencken: A Life* provides a comprehensive and insightful biography.[1]

Mencken's correspondent was Philip Goodman, who was born in Philadelphia, five years Mencken's junior, in 1885. Goodman left his middle-class German-Jewish roots and the duller life of Philadelphia to settle in New York in 1905. The bustling, cosmopolitan city proved to be perfect for Goodman. He set up a New York advertising agency, and made a considerable success, representing garment-district merchants from his office at 33rd Street and Broadway. He was at home equally among businessmen, the artistic set, and the travelers he met on annual trips to Europe. He loved entertaining, good food and drink, and the spirited disputation that followed.

Goodman entered the lives of H. L. Mencken and George Jean Nathan in 1917. Mencken and Nathan had been joint editors of *The Smart Set* since 1914, and were consequently full of material for books that could be pasted together from the best things they had written in the magazine. Goodman, looking for new fields to conquer, proposed to begin publishing their books in popular editions—to sell for 90 cents in drugstores. Mencken and Nathan were hoping to find a publisher who would take more interest in their books and Goodman seemed to offer promise.

By 1918 Goodman had published *Damn! A Book of Calumny* and *In Defense of Women* for Mencken, and *Bottoms Up* and *A Book Without a Title* for Nathan. Goodman as publisher, perhaps oddly for an advertising agent, was weak in the area of

1. Fred Hobson, *Mencken: A Life* (New York: Random House, 1994).

Philip Goodman's bookshop logotype appeared
in the books he published for Mencken.

promotion; the books were not finding a market. Mencken recalls that even "an inflammatory circular" and the books' pro-
vocative titles didn't work.[2] Soon Mencken decided on Alfred
A. Knopf as his publisher, but the Mencken-Goodman friendship continued, and even blossomed, without the irritation of
an unsuccessful business connection.

In the 1920s Goodman became an overnight success as a
Broadway producer. He turned Don Marquis' newspaper column, *The Old Soak*, into a dramatic hit and followed in 1923
with *Poppy*, the musical that launched W. C. Fields into a new
career as a comic actor.[3] As Mencken notes in his introduction

2. H. L. Mencken, *My Life as Author and Editor* (New York: Knopf, 1993),
228.

3. The Old Soak, a bibulous philosopher, was a favorite with New Yorkers
for such wisdom as: "I'd rather have Despair combined with a case of Bourbon
liquor than all the Hope in the world by itself."

to his correspondence with Goodman, Goodman's hits "played to big business, and by 1923 he was full of money."[4]

During the twenties, Philip Goodman and H. L. Mencken met regularly for meals and drinks; in fact, Mencken notes, "I saw more of him than of any other man in New York."[5] At the beginning of Prohibition, Goodman found sources of good beer in New Jersey, which became the destination of many malty excursions "to drink the waters," as Mencken always quipped. Mencken regularly visited Goodman's home in New York, and Goodman came to Baltimore to visit the Saturday Night Club. They were not only dining together; from 1918 on they maintained an extensive correspondence between New York and Baltimore.

The Goodman-Mencken correspondence was often about business, and sometimes about the events of that turbulent time, but just as often the letters featured wholly imaginary stories. This is the most playful, the most outrageous, flowering of Mencken's letter-writing career. The joyous story-telling in these letters, a continuation of the tall tales the men told each other over dinner and drinks, was different from Mencken's other epistolary hijinks in both volume and exuberance. Seeing the promise in these letters, the correspondents planned to edit them into a book, to be called "Do You Remember?" The book was never completed, however, because other projects occupied both men throughout the 1920s.

It is evident from their letters that the men loved, and wished to recreate, the special world German immigrants

4. H. L. Mencken, introduction (dated 1941) to "Letters to Philip Goodman, 1918–1933," in the Enoch Pratt Free Library, Baltimore.

5. Mencken, *My Life as Author and Editor*, 226.

When in exuberant mood Mencken decorated his correspondence with
a *Seidel* of beer. (Drawing from *Dreiser-Mencken Letters*, ed. Thomas P.
Riggio [Philadelphia: University of Pennsylvania Press, 1986], 1:167.

found in America in the 1880s and 1890s. The period they had
known as children was magical, and they could see by 1917
that it would never again be possible. That innocence and old-
world charm had already disappeared by the twenties. Both
men missed the boisterous middle-class German society that
had so amply nourished their childhood.

The immigrant families that Goodman and Mencken knew
were intimately connected to their society and to city life. They
were in singing clubs, bundts, unions, political organizations,
fraternal lodges, building societies, sewing circles, sporting and
recreational clubs, congregations, and schools. They had spouses,
cousins, lovers, friends, coworkers, next-door neighbors, school-
mates, suppliers, customers, barbers, and the people they met
regularly at their neighborhood bar. Their ties went both directions across the Atlantic: they sent money to Chemnitz and
expected new relatives to arrive from Darmstadt.

Since these letters deal with the experiences of immigrant families in a new land, some stories feature people who fall upon hard times. Oddly, to our eyes, these people do not immediately receive what we call welfare. Instead, we see that cases of need are routinely handled by churches, synagogues, and benevolent societies. Mencken writes about the Knights of Pythias (March 1918) and Goodman writes to Mencken about the Pershing Sick Benefit Society (April 1918). Benefits paid to members of these societies are theirs by right—they have a contract with the society. Goodman's letter tells the story of how that right was enforced by a lawsuit.

The members of a benevolent society paid a small weekly fee and in return were guaranteed sick benefits, a proper funeral, and a small amount of life insurance. The societies branched out to provide a welter of other services, including adult education, orphanages, homes for the aged, and doctors. Some societies started their own retail businesses and banks. One of the great benefits was that the benevolent society usually spoke one's native language, in the case of these immigrants, German or Yiddish.

We can well understand that beyond a simple admission of failure, going on general relief was an embarrassment in these early days because it was clear evidence of a social, even more than an economic, disorder. Every family had the occasional stumble. But to go on welfare meant that you did not belong to a support group, and that meant for all practical purposes that you were an outcast.

In cases of need, any normal member of society looked to his family, church, union, lodge, and benevolent society. With each of these sources of support the needy family had a formal or informal contract for help when it was truly needed. Many middle-class families had bolstered their position by membership in more than one benevolent society—fraternal order, union, or religious group. Not to have these social ties meant that one had cut off ties to the wider society, and this was usually only true of those few people who had decided to make a new start on the frontier.

Finally, a word about the exuberant whimsy to follow. Most episodes in the letters are designed to be humorous, at least to someone who shares Mencken and Goodman's view of the world. Mencken had already published an earnest volume of letters airing his differences with a socialist aristocrat;[6] this is not such a book. Mencken later tried writing a book with George Jean Nathan, to be called "Two Editors," which would expound their critical view of contemporary America. This is not that type of book, either. This is a book of nostalgic whimsy.

When Mencken and Goodman write to each other, every day is April Fool's Day. Not only are most of the characters fictitious, but the writers frequently state the exact opposite of their true opinions. Mencken writes matter-of-factly about utter implausibilities. Goodman adopts a style of simple, naïve credulity while describing religion, and even professes to being a Catholic when the mood strikes him. Goodman is unmatched, as Mencken noted, in his effective descriptions of human bathos.

There are generally several layers of humor present in any

6. Robert Rives La Monte and H. L. Mencken, *Men Versus the Man* (New York: Henry Holt, 1910).

story. There is the obvious fun in outlandish German names and there is a more complex humor in the American corruption of these names. The names sometimes have been chosen to describe the character of the person, what we call "speaking names." Then there is the plot: activities that are gently humorous in depicting the tastes of a simpler time or more pointed in poking fun at unsophisticated rural folk who find themselves in the city. These simple people would eventually have had to come to terms with the industrial world even had they stayed in Europe, but the immigrants made a double jump: into a new country and into modern, urban life.

Added to these layers of humor, Goodman and Mencken, as storytellers, take us back to hear the tales the immigrants told, and the scrapes they got into. And, better, we hear their reactions to the events of their lives, giving us a deeper look into their motivations, and a better appreciation of the kind of people they were.

The storytellers adopt a credulous tone, merely reporting the stories as they heard them. Of course we understand that Mencken and Goodman are superior to the protagonists, gently mocking their pretensions and foibles. But at a deeper level we sense that the storytellers love these simple people who were, after all, their grandparents.

So, what is the point of this whimsical correspondence, mounting up—in a little more than two years—to a small book? The underlying theme, it seems, is human pretension. Mencken and Goodman are extolling the commonplace virtues: good beer, good cooking, knowing your craft, expressing feelings honestly. They extol common sense. They blast the tendency of common folk to raise heroes to absurd heights and to let powerful people do their thinking for them, when the common people should instead trust themselves. It is an individualist message, this pulling-down of icons.

Time and again the letters mention outstanding examples of human fallibility. The references are so subtle that a careless reader will miss them. A dinner is held for a hero, but he is actually a cowardly general. A cigar is named for a senator, but he was thrown out of the Senate in disgrace. The president of a great university turns out to be an autocratic poseur. Again and again we meet charlatans, and they always seem to have an army of admirers.

The moral is that human fallibility will always make a mock of human pretension. Goodman and Mencken remind us that the simple pleasures and common virtues are best.

The dedication of this book expresses the sentiments of the authors. On May 2, 1933, Mencken wrote to Goodman, "It is grand news that Lily is so much better. I needn't send our love: she knows what Sara and I think of her. All men have better wives than they deserve."

A Note on Methodology

These letters present a problem to the modern reader for several reasons. First, they discuss the current news of 1918 and 1919—just yesterday to the correspondents, but seven decades removed from us. Moreover, the letters delve into the 1880s and 1890s, the fondly remembered childhood years of Mencken and Goodman, but foreign territory to the modern reader.

The correspondents derive special joy, of course, from sharing these memories and describing their favorite things, and season the stew with their inside jokes, but they leave us out. As a result of my decision to annotate the text extensively, I inevitably will explain things that are obvious to some readers but, I trust, not to all. Younger readers will have little knowledge of World War I or the literary figures at the turn of the century. As for German unification, of intense interest at that time, I have added brief explanations because it now is almost forgotten.

I have translated a great many foreign words, perhaps too many, but I have followed the wisdom of Mark Twain, who expressed my reasoning in *A Tramp Abroad:* "I have a prejudice against people who print things in a foreign language and add no translation. When I am the reader, and the author considers me able to do the translating myself, he pays me quite a nice compliment—but if he would do the translating for me I would try and get along without the compliment."[7]

Mencken and Goodman used their favorite German words as though the words had entered the English language, and indeed many of them had. English, the language that has borrowed more words than any other, was borrowing German vocabulary wholesale. And no wonder: Germans amounted to as many as one-third of the immigrants to this country, and German universities, authors, and sciences were at a peak of prestige.

German words that had apparently entered the American language by 1917 had just as decisively left it a generation later. During World War I there was a concerted effort to rid common speech of anything that sounded German, and the

7. Mark Twain, *A Tramp Abroad* (1880), 60.

German language itself, previously taught in many public schools, was removed from the curriculum. It was no longer patriotic to say "sauerkraut"—it was now "liberty cabbage"; words less common than "sauerkraut" simply disappeared.

The effect of this on the letters that follow is that many words that look German were in fact used by the correspondents as English; they felt that the words were part of the commonly used and understood language.

Finally, a word about my role as editor. More than is usually the case, I have had to be an active editor and to make choices about the style and positioning of material—choices that would better have been made by Goodman and Mencken if they were here. Mencken himself tried to "amalgamate and edit" the letters, but found that, "as they stand, the letters are too sketchy and chaotic."[8] He was right. There was a lot of work to be done and the only way I could do it was to step boldly into the shoes of the original writers and make the choices I felt they would have made.

I did not start from a clean manuscript, nor from anything that was typed by either of the correspondents. I started with material that was not the original letters, but Goodman's secretary's excerpts from the correspondence, inaccurately typed. Only one excerpt even bears a date. She did not know German, and did not understand the references that were made in the letters.

I was in the position of a cinema director who finds himself with a barrel of film clips that must be spliced together into a story. Two distinguished cameramen had shot these scenes,

8. Mencken to Goodman, February 23, 1919.

and my job was to allow their genius to come to the screen. This was the only way I could realize the original vision of Goodman and Mencken. I needed to be an extraordinarily conscientious editor to allow their genius to shine, and, I often thought, a brazen one even to try.

My task was to reconstitute the correspondence that was preserved in the volume of excerpts called "Extracts from Letters between H. L. Mencken and Philip Goodman," in the Enoch Pratt Free Library, using a procedure that I describe more fully in the preface. The men created the great bulk of "Do You Remember?" in 1918 and 1919, and in 1919 Goodman sent Mencken the first set of excerpts. As more letters came along Goodman added to the collection and sent a second set of pages to Mencken, including the material back to 1918. The second set, amounting to 149 excerpts, constitutes the volume we see today in the Mencken Room. "In 1920 or 1921," Mencken notes, "he [Goodman] prepared the following extracts with a view to making a book of the correspondence, but the project was never carried out."[9]

I supplied dates for the letters as accurately as can be known. In cases where dates are not typed on the letters but are known or can be deduced, I have included them in brackets. In cases where Mencken's letters had been preserved in "Letters to Philip Goodman, 1918–1933," in the Enoch Pratt Free Library, I used the dates where given. There was the one date that Goodman's secretary had supplied. In all other cases I ordered the letters as well as I could.

9. Mencken's prefatory note (dated July 1941) to "Extracts from Letters between H. L. Mencken and Philip Goodman," in the Enoch Pratt Free Library, Baltimore.

The Mencken Room. (Courtesy Enoch Pratt Free Library.)

In some cases the excerpts were too short to use, and like a cinema director I had to leave a little of the film on the floor. Here is an example of an unusable excerpt: "Gustav is now bookkeeper at the Goldbrau Brewery, and Anna takes in sewing." And another: "Schuft. He bought his paper collars by the box, 'Sweet Evalina.'" Where small bits of material did not fit into any story I had to let them go. I took comfort in the realization that even productions of Shakespeare leave some lines unspoken.

But my chief exercise was not choosing what to leave out. On the contrary, it was to decide which parts of the correspondence to bring in. The full texts of some of the letters appear in "Letters to Philip Goodman, 1918–1933." I felt that the joint publishing venture—*Damn! A Book of Calumny* and *In Defense of Women*—was interesting as a backdrop to their friendship and was worthy of a fuller treatment. For instance, the letter of October 2, 1918, received not only a date but also its first paragraph from my examination of the fuller texts.

Unfortunately, neither the full texts prepared by Mencken's secretary, nor the excerpts typed by Goodman's secretary, may be considered authoritative. Both are far from complete. Both have obvious errors of transcription and the full texts of the letters carry partial, and sometimes incorrect, dates. Mencken's secretary even goes so far as to correct his off-color language! In the absence of an authoritative text, I had to exercise judgment in reconstituting the original letters.

In matters of style, I modernized spellings in some areas, and left them in the original form elsewhere. I was in the position of wanting neither to efface the authentic style of the writers, nor to offend the eye of the modern reader. As an example of modernization, "to-day" became "today." In addition, standard conventions of our own day are used with regard to punctuation and numerals. I have also corrected typographical and spelling errors and have standardized their German. When I found obvious errors of transcription I silently corrected them. The ellipsis points in the text were a part of the original letters and are used to suggest a progression of thought when it would be less elegant to spell it out.

In only one case did I find a passage that I felt Mencken and Goodman would have removed because of changing cultural mores. I excised Mencken's story that "Dr. Max Kuprin has been put in charge of the anti-cootie campaign in the public schools of the Italian Quarter."[10] In their age, use of ethnic

10. Mencken to Goodman, August 7, 1919.

stereotypes was common, but I believe the writers, if working on their book today, would follow present-day practice, omitting what would be a pointless affront.

Where it has been necessary to maintain the tone of the story, I have preserved the original orthography. You will find that some common nouns are capitalized as they would be if they were German. The writers adopted idiosyncratic capitalization as a reference to the Old World, which they were, after all, remembering. It was also a reference to an older style in this country; the U.S. Constitution, for example, was written to "secure the Blessings of Liberty to ourselves and our Posterity."

Names appearing in the letters are fictitious. Except for a few historical persons who are identified in my notes, no reference is made to any actual person.

German Names

Goodman and Mencken appreciated German ethnic names, and built about three hundred of them into the text of the "Do You Remember?" letters. They liked the sound of the names and found their historical meanings fascinating. Many of these meanings are listed below.

First, though, a word about popular etymology, or folk etymology, of names. Folk etymology is the common understanding of the origin of a word. This commonly understood, or misunderstood, meaning of a name is of more importance in these letters than the historical derivation. For instance, Mencken and Goodman introduce us to a Frau Schauffle, who is a paragon of the common virtues. The name means "shovel," or "a shovel-maker," which is a good fit for the frau's humble station. It is this common understanding that we care about, and not a history of the name that may point to a different original meaning. In addition, thinking of Frau Schauffle, we may consider other related names, for instance, Schnabel (snout, talkative one) and Schnauffer (snorter).

Names last for centuries, while the language changes. The origins of Old Germanic names were largely forgotten centuries ago, a fact that has continued to pose riddles for the users of the names. One response is to change the spelling of the name to match a current word.

Sometimes the spelling of a name changes over time to make it conform to what is perceived to be the basis of the name, while all memory of the original form is forgotten. We cannot, therefore, be sure that the commonly accepted meaning of a name is its historical root.

The folk perception is still important, however. When Goodman and Mencken use names in the letters of this book they are likely to be thinking about the names in the same way that any normal German would. The name Lahm, for instance, suggests "lame," and one would suppose that an ancestor of the family that bears the name was indeed lame, but this could be wrong. There are a dozen other places that the name could originate, including portions of other German words, and these words may have been changed slightly over time. It should be noted that the same name can have different forms within Germany; the Low German names Kock, Groote, and Schaper are the High German names Koch, Grosse, and Schaefer.

Many languages contributed to the German name pool. In particular, infusions of names came from Slavic and Latin countries. Moltke, the family name of the great German general, comes from Slavic, meaning "young." The Latin word *caupo*, for "merchant," becomes Kauf and Kaufmann. The Latin *molinarius* gives us Mueller or Miller.

With rare exceptions, and these are annotated in the text, the characters in the narrative are fictional. Mencken and Goodman, have, however, given their characters typical German-American adventures, and typical German-American names. Here you will see the marvelous range of names that the immigrants brought from dozens of parts of German-speaking Europe. Today, German is the tenth-most spoken language, surpassing French and Italian, a consequence of the fact that it is spoken in a wide range of European locations.

The naming conventions of these many communities are represented in the stories, with fascinating results. Here you will find, among others, the following names (with their meanings): Aal (eel), Adels (noble), Albers (poplar tree), Altmeier (proprietor), Arnheim (eagle hamlet), Bauernschmidt (village smith), Berghoff (mountain farm), Bernau (swamp meadow), Biebl (Bible), Biederbeck (boundary brook), Bierbauer (beer brewer), Bischoff (bishop), Bleimuller (lead worker), Brautwein (wedding wine), Brobst (provost), Buchholtz (beechwood), Buchsbaum (boxwood), Buddenbohm (bog-tree), Busch (tavernkeeper, a reference to the practice of hanging a branch over the tavern door), Decker or Dekker (roofer), Dieffenbach (deep brook), Dingledein (hammerer of blades), Dittenhocfcr (swampy farm), Doernblatter (thicket), Ebberle (little wild boar), Ehrlich (honest), Eichenlaub (oak folliage), Eisenbrandt (iron and fire combine to indicate smith).

And more: Eisenlohr (smith), Eisner (ironmonger), Falk

(falcon or falconer), Freihofer (independent farmer), Gast (guest, stranger), Gegner (opponent), Geiger (fiddler), Gelb (blond), Gerstbach (Gerhard's brook), Gieseke (brilliant scion), Ginsberg (Gunther's mountain), Glaenzer (shining), Goldblatt (gold leaf), Grieb (living in a hollow), Gritzmann (grain dealer), Groscholz (large wood), Haas (hare), Habig (hawk), Hagedorn (hawthorn), Hahn (rooster), Hartfeldter (stag field), Helbling (ha'penny), Hetzel (beater on a hunt), Hirschbein (deer bone), Hochschild (high shield), Hofmeister (manager of a cloister), Holtzmann (woodsman), Horst (thicket), Hufnagel (blacksmith, shoer of horses), Kaplan (chaplain), Kessler (kettle maker), Klopstuck (beating stick), Klugmann (clever), Knochenhauer (butcher), Kruger (tavern keeper), Kuehnle (brave man), Lachner (lives on a lake), Lahm (lame), Lastner (burden carrier), Lilienthal (lily valley), Lindauer (swampy meadow), Linsenmeyer (lentil farmer), Loeffler (spoon maker), Lohmann (forester), Mandelbaum (almond tree), Moll (heavy-set), Moltke (young), Oberholtzer (beyond the forest).

And still more: Oehlenschläger (threshing bat for seed oil), Ortman (dwells at end of village), Ostertag (Easter), Pfaelzer (from the Palatinate), Pfannenbecker (cake baker), Potthast (pot roast), Pulvermacher (powder-maker), Raab (raven), Roesser (swamp, a name for a farm), Rosenblatt (rose leaf), Rosenzweig (rose branch), Rothgeb (advice giver), Saalberg (blessed mountain), Saltzmann (salt seller), Sauerwein (sour wine), Schaeffer (shepherd), Schaffner (manager), Schandt (disgrace), Scharnagel (a poker for ashes), Schaumloeffels (foam-skimming spoon), Scheidt (wood cutter), Schiff (ship), Schildt (shield), Schlegel (turnkey), Schlegelmilch (buttermilk, milk dealer), Schnabel (snout, talkative one), Schneider (tailor), Schnittkin (reaper), Schnur (string maker), Schuetz (marksman), Schuldenfrei (debt-free farm), Schultheis (magistrate), Schweickhardt (cattle farmer), Schweinfurth (swamp ford), Schwoerer (swearer), Semmel (baker of white bread), Sitzer (sitter), Spaeth (late), Spangenberg (swamp mountain), Stegmaier (farmer near footpath), Steiner (stone worker), Stiefelbaum (boot tree), Strauss (fight), Stroebel (disheveled), Strohmeyer (straw dealer), Stumpff (blunt), Tiefenthaler (deep valley), Traubmann (vintner), Ulrich (inherited property), Unterkircher (lower church), Unverzagt (undaunted), Walden (forests), Weniger (fewer), Widmaier (pasture farmer), Winterfeldt (winter field), Wirt (proprietor), Wohl (wool), Wohlgemuth (happy disposition), Wolff (wolf), Zimmermann (carpenter), and Zorn (anger).

Goodman and Mencken liked to use these strikingly ethnic names to add flavor to the pieces and because they recalled the names with affection. In some cases the attributions of meanings indeed seem to derive from folk etymology and the spelling of the name changes to match the new folk explanation. In any case, there is a general understanding that the names are related to the roots listed here, and Mencken and Goodman may well have used this folk wisdom in assigning names to the characters or in appreciating the name itself and wanting to use it in the story.

I have noted cases where the name has apparently been chosen to fit the character—what is called a "speaking name." In most cases, however, there is no connection between the meaning of the name and the character. Some names associated particularly with many Jewish immigrants (Gottlob, Berkovitz,

Kaplan) have been chosen to fit the characters in a story involving Jews.

Some German names are contractions of better-known originals, such as Baltz (Balthasar), Bartels or Bartsch (Bartholomaeus), Behrends or Bentz (Bernard), Borchardt (Burkhart), Ebbecke (Eggebrecht), Garthe or Goerst (Gerhard), Goeckel (Gottfried), Hempel (Hambrecht), Hoerle (Hermann), Koontz or Kuntz (Conrad), Muth (Helmuth), Seibold (Siegbalt), Sigel (Siegfried), Theiss (Matthias), and Volz (Volkmar).

Mencken and Anti-Semitism

For several years the national press has carried sensational articles about the supposed anti-Semitism of H. L. Mencken. The topic is especially relevant to this book, because Philip Goodman was Jewish, and eventually came to a break with Mencken in part because of the latter's refusal to appreciate the threat that Germany in the 1930s posed to Jews in Europe.

Anti-Semitism, if present in these letters, would raise many questions for the reader. Mencken and Goodman are not only best friends, exchanging letters on a daily basis, but also discuss the world as though they were actual cousins. Aunt Tillie and Uncle Fritz, who appear and reappear in these letters, are presented by Mencken and Goodman as their actual aunt and uncle.

What are we to make of this? If Mencken were anti-Semitic, why would Philip Goodman be his closest friend? Arguably, his best friend early in his career was George Jean Nathan and at the end of his career Alfred A. Knopf, his publisher, both Jewish. What's going on here?

In Mencken's time anti-Semitism meant hating Jews or wishing harm to them. This never applied to Mencken. At one point in this lengthy correspondence, Mencken responds to Goodman's criticism of Jews with the observation, "You are more anti-Semitic than I am." In fact they could joke about the issue because they knew that to be an *actual* anti-Semite would be, in a fundamental sense, to take leave of one's reason.

As the term is used today, anti-Semitism also encompasses those who make harsh generalizations about Jews, and Mencken makes these generalizations in his writings. Therefore, there is a temptation to consider Mencken, in our super-sensitive age, an anti-Semite. Goodman makes similar harsh generalizations, but he—as a Jew—is presumptively not an anti-Semite, even when he criticizes Jews.

If making harsh generalizations qualifies one as prejudiced, Mencken also was prejudiced against politicians, professors, theologians, journalists, southerners, northerners, blacks, whites, men, and women. At one time or other he wrote harshly against every group, including, most vociferously, Anglo-Saxons, and even his own German-Americans.

But a person who speaks harshly about *every* group is not properly described as an anti-Semite. The name for this person is misanthrope. In the same way, someone who excoriates each religion in its turn might sensibly be called an atheist, and we would not stop to point out his objection to, say, fundamentalists. We have not identified a central tenet of Mencken's philosophy when we say that he spoke harshly of Jews.

In our age, to be an anti-Semite means that you prefer some group that is supposedly superior to Jews. Commonly, it is some half-understood "Aryan" or "Nordic" race. If someone wants to tar Mencken with the brush of anti-Semitism, it is only reasonable that as a part of the charge he tell us which group Mencken preferred. But you will not find such a group. In fact, when comparing Jews and Gentiles, Mencken usually comes out in favor of the Jews.

The pervading anti-Semitism of this century is too well known to require much elaboration here. Jews were kept out of colleges, professions, business firms, clubs, and neighborhoods. They were unable to get articles accepted in magazines. They could not play for professional baseball teams. Wall Street firms would not hire them. Law firms told them they could never be promoted to partnership. We know about this preju- dice, and Mencken was not part of it. He chose Jews as his busi- ness associates. As we have seen, his closest friends were Jews. He published Jewish writers enthusiastically in his magazines.

One of Mencken's best-known newspaper articles, entitled "Help for the Jews," appeared in November 1938. In it, Mencken suggested that the Roosevelt administration should relax immigration quotas for the Jews trapped in Europe. "Why shouldn't the United States take in a couple of hundred thousand . . . or even all of them?" he asked. His appeal was to no avail because the Roosevelt administration felt that admit- ting Jews would be unpopular.

Privately, though, Mencken was more successful. He wrote letters for, and personally sponsored, at least a dozen relatives of Jewish friends, Jews who were fleeing Europe in 1938 and 1939. These were depression years and not everyone was in a position to help, but Mencken clearly did so. After the refugees reached America, he took a personal interest in seeing them get settled and some became his friends. The full story is in Fred Hobson's biography of Mencken.[11]

When Mencken's supporters in the present day produce all of the above evidence, evidence that convinced Mencken's friends that he was not an anti-Semite, one final argument inevitably comes up: Mencken used the word "kike."

In 1989 it was discovered that Mencken used the word "kikes" in his diary. This fact, supposedly proving that Mencken was an anti-Semite, was trumpeted in the national press for weeks. It well may be that there is today no innocent use of what has become a racial epithet, but in Mencken's day Jews themselves used the term. Mencken used the word the way Jews did; in fact, he used it with his Jewish friends. No one was offended; they all knew what "kike" meant. The word apparently originated in the Jewish community itself as a reference to later immigrants who were offensive or lacked social skills. An offensive Jew was judged to be a kike because of his actions. Use of the word did not disparage or even refer to *all* Jews. In the same way today we use the term "redneck" or "skinhead" to describe people of a certain antisocial behavior and attitude, but no one supposes that we are speaking of *all* white people.

A word used within an ethnic group may become an unpleasant name for the group itself. "Polack" is simply the name Polish people apply to themselves, but now is used by others as a slur. "Wop," from *guappo*, a Neapolitan word meaning a dandy or fop, was used disparagingly by Italians themselves before it was adopted by a wider audience. "Kike" is certainly not an isolated instance.

11. Hobson, *Mencken*, x, xv–xvi, 168–70, 422–25.

It is argued that today the word "kike" is only used by un-couth people, and it attacks all Jews. Today's reader hates to see the word, and is offended. Ergo, Mencken must have been an anti-Semite. This goes farther than judging Mencken by today's heightened sensibilities; we are asked to judge Mencken by his use of a word that today has no innocent ap-plication. First we forget that the language of the time was not as circumspectly sensitive as we would prefer; then we forget the earlier meaning of the word itself. This raises polemic to the point of character assassination. One wonders about the health of scholarly inquiry in our day when we see that this type of attack is characteristic of contemporary writing.

Put simply, people who knew Mencken best, and many of these were Jews, thought of him as a good person, and not—by any definition that *they* would have used—an anti-Semite.

THE
"DO YOU REMEMBER?"
LETTERS

[January 1918]

Dear Mencken:

In going over some old papers recently I discovered the Program of the occasion of the visit of Gen. Franz Segal[1] to the

---

1. Franz Sigel (1824–1902) was a Union general in the War Between the States, and an inspiration to German-Americans. As the most popular German in America at the time, he was an important factor in enlisting German immigrants on the Union side. "I fights mit Sigel" became a byword. But Goodman, a keen observer of human character, enjoyed heroic figures with equivocal records. Mencken scholar Richard Schrader believes that Goodman is here "satirizing a blowhard general in Twainian fashion." Sigel was given his command less for his skills as a soldier than to make Lincoln popular among German immigrants. Indeed, Sigel's notable military engagements often resulted in defeat. Despite this, he continued to be a hero to the German-American population, who feted him at dinners and years later honored him with an equestrian statue on Manhattan's Riverside Drive. The Germans' continued veneration of their hero, in the face of his ineptitude, was an instance of the uncomplicated faith of simple folk. This story is the first of many in which we meet the good-hearted immigrants who brought charity, warmth, and a large measure of credulity, to America.

Humboldt Lodge No. 351 A. F. & A. M.[2] in your city on the night of Jan. 23d, 1889. Dr. Schneider delivered the invocation. The General was introduced by the Grand Master, Dr. Barnett Benswanger. Those who served on the Honorary Committee were Christian Zwilling, Henry Vogel, Ludwig Jaeger, Fred Brobst, Jakob Schauffle and Otto Weitzenkorn.[3] Music was rendered by Woehr's String Orchestra "specially augmented for the occasion." A very touching ceremony was the presentation to the General of the *Jahrbuch*[4] containing the portraits of all the members, bound by Ferdinand Busch in white morocco with very intricate gold tooling.

The General started his address of acceptance by saying, "I shall always count this night as one of the greatest moments of my life." He delivered the speech holding the huge volume in his right arm. But, according to Chris Zwilling, the big moment of the evening was yet to come. When the General was escorted to the Grand Banquet Room by Chris himself, he found it dark, each member standing with one foot on his chair and the other on the table with his glass raised, the faint light from an adjoining room striking the upraised glasses and giving the effect of a crystal grotto. Chris always averred that the idea was his, but Kuno Kirschbaum claimed that it was he who

2. "A. F. & A. M.": Ancient Free and Accepted Masons, freemasons. Baron Alexander von Humboldt (1769–1859) was one of the greatest German scientists.

3. These names have a thoroughly German flavor. Benswanger (reed field) and Schauffle (shovel-maker) are of the Swabian dialect. Zwilling means "twin," Weitzenkorn is wheat.

4. *Jahrbuch:* Yearbook.

really originated the scheme. It must have been a great sight. God, how I would like to have been there!

All, all are gone, the old familiar faces. But we've all got to pass Adam Dieterich's place some day without getting out.[5] When Chris's time came the Humboldt gave him a great send-off. I counted thirty-one carriages. The white-aproned cortege at the cemetery was an impressive spectacle. Adelbert Hahlo, afterward assistant District Attorney, was the Grand Master at the time and his sermon at the grave was a profound and scholarly address, liberally sprinkled with quotations from Bohn's best books.[6] He started with the words, "Man is but a grain of sand on life's vast desert," when a horse nearby began neighing and drowned out the rest of it. I afterward asked him if he could send me a written copy, but he wrote back regretting that he could not inasmuch as the address was delivered spontaneously, as all such addresses should be, adding that all of his Masonic Sermons were rendered without the slightest preparation beforehand. Well might old Mrs. Hahlo say, as she did so frequently, "My Adelbert is so smart that I'm always afraid something'll happen to him." Of course we know that nothing will happen to him. There is a Special Providence that looks after such as Adelbert.

Goodman

5. To pass Adam Dieterich's place "without getting out" means to be in a coffin. Dieterich's *Gasthaus* or inn was on the way to the cemetery. The mourners would stop there for refreshment after services.

6. "Bohn's best books": Henry George Bohn (1796–1884), son of a German bookbinder, settled in London and became a book dealer. He published editions of standard works, so that by reading the Bohn "Libraries" one could become educated in the classics. Eventually there were 766 volumes of Bohn's books.

Dear Goodman:

I announce with profound sorrow the death of Martin Meyerdirck. He left $5,000 to the orphan asylum, and many thousands to other worthy objects.

But I blush for you. What is to be thought of a man who turns the name of Major General Franz Sigel into Segal? Why not go the whole hog and make it Seagull? I was too young, of course, to be present at the banquet in Raine's Hall, when the general was entertained by Humboldt Lodge, but I well remember the evening he was the guest of honor at a Wine *Kommers* given by the Metzger *Liedertafel*, with Prof. Dr. Gustav Raabe in the chair.[7] I have it from Fritz Buchsbaum, who had the catering contract, that the assembled bibuli drank 700 bottles of Erbacher[8]—say 3.6 bottles to a man. The general made a speech lasting from 10:05 to nearly 2:00 A.M. and recounted in detail the whole story of his invasion of the Valley of Virginia, forgetting nothing.[9] At one point he drew out

7. *Kommers:* Social meeting or students' drinking bout. *Liedertafel:* Choral society.

8. Erbacher: An esteemed white Rhine wine.

9. The Valley of Virginia refers to Sigel's defeat at New Market. Mencken shows that he has recognized Goodman's jest; he allows Sigel to recall his most humiliating battle. In May 1864, General Grant sent Sigel off with superior forces to capture the Shenandoah Valley. Sigel quickly lost at New Market and retreated at record pace down the valley to Strasburg. When Grant asked how Sigel was progressing, General Halleck reported acidly that Sigel "is already in full retreat on Strasburg. . . . He will do nothing but run. Never did anything else." New Market was especially vexing because the soldiers who turned the tide against Sigel were the young cadets of the Virginia Military Institute. To this day, Sigel's detractors chide him for "losing to the

a parchment and read the complete roster of his brigade. Here, however, he hunched a bit. That is, when he came to the Schmidts, for example, he simply said thirty-nine Schmidts, and didn't read their front names. Two of his staff officers, *Oberstleutnant* Himmelheber and *Oberstabsarzt* Gusdorff, were also present.[10] Both grew mellow and shed tears.

But more of this anon. I am sweating on a ms. for a publisher of your name.[11] Maybe you know him: a fellow of matronly habit, an ale drinker. One night lately he drank George Nathan[12] under the table. But does it take any talent to drink George Nathan under the table? I doubt it. I'd like to match him against a real professor—for example, Hermann Schlens.

Mencken

My Dear Mencken:

There was a feast of reason and a flow of soul at Max Oberholtzer's last night upon the occasion of a farewell dinner to young Max, who has just been called to the colors.[13] Only the relatives and a few intimate friends were present. Max, who

---

cadets." To give Sigel his due, he often proved his physical courage on the battlefield, and he would not ask his men to throw their lives into an effort to salvage a bad situation. Add to this a talent for politics, and it is easy to explain his continuing popularity among German-Americans.

10. *Oberstleutnant:* Lieutenant-colonel. *Oberstabsarzt:* Major in the medical service.

11. Mencken was pasting together *Damn! A Book of Calumny* for Goodman, drawing upon his *Smart Set* articles.

12. George Jean Nathan, famous theater critic, was coeditor with Mencken of *The Smart Set* at this time.

13. "called to the colors": Drafted as a soldier in World War I.

was in class One-A, sat at the head of the table between his Mama and Papa, and bowed his head in conscious pride when Dr. Kleinschmidt referred to him as the valiant young hero who, like the warrior of old, went off to give combat to the foe.

It was a very touching address, the Doctor going into the details of how when Max made three attempts to have his classification changed and was each time overruled by his local board, thereby showing the country's great need for his services, he shouldered his musket as became a son of Max Oberholtzer, himself a soldier in his youth. Mrs. Stumpff, an aunt, wept like a child and had to be led from the room. Another very beautiful tribute was paid to the lad by Emil Doernblatter, recently elected to the Assembly. Doernblatter took for his text that line from Luther, "Great heroes are especial gifts of God." He drew a parallel between young Max and the great reformer, showing how each was a cavalier of his own conscience.

Max will leave for camp today and with him will go the soldier's drinking cup that belonged to his grandfather and which has remained in the family for so many years. The formal presentation was made by his father with the words, "Let it serve as a star in guiding you in the righteousness of your cause." The cup was then passed around and on it I observed the inscription: "Sadowa, July 3, 1866."[14]

Goodman

14. Sadowa, July 3, 1866, was a key battle in the Seven Weeks' War between Prussia and Austria. In the battle the Prussian soldiers held fast against overwhelming odds and by the end of the day had turned the tide against the Austrian army. The war was deliberately provoked by Bismarck as one step toward the unification of Germany.

H. L. Mencken, *c.* 1908; photo by Janvier, Baltimore. The young editor, already displaying his mature powers, was beginning his reviews for *The Smart Set*. These labors brought him to the attention of aspiring publisher Philip Goodman. (Corbis-Bettmann.)

Jan. 23 [1918]

Dear Goodman:

I'll do my best with the book.[15] It is no easy job. I have already got it under way.

15. The book was published with Goodman's inflammatory title, *Damn! A Book of Calumny*. In a marginal note on this letter Mencken says, "The title of the book will be 'Forty-Nine Little Essays,'" but Goodman prevailed in the choice of title.

Your remarks regarding Dreiser and Huneker[16] convince me that you are an even worse critic than I am. You remind me of the late Kuno Kirschbaum—but that is another story. Dr. Garfinkle is not related to the Garfinkles from Elberfeldt. Imagine an Elberfeldt Garfinkle closing down a factory!

Yours in Xt.,[17] *Mencken*

Dear Mencken:

Among the 40,000 slackers[18] held up here on Monday was Tascha Margolin, Assistant Editor of "To-Morrow"[19] and a

---

16. Theodore Dreiser (1871–1945) and James Gibbons Huneker (1860–1921) were Mencken's friends as well as literary and artistic collaborators. Their discussions with Mencken, later including Goodman, equipped Mencken with facts and attitudes essential to his career as a critic. Huneker was the more important influence, as he provided a virtual encyclopedia of European culture, together with the earthy stories about historic personages that made a malty bout memorable. Some of the historic figures to appear in these letters first appeared in monologues by Huneker, delivered over tankards of Pilsner. Mencken was never shy about recalling the torrent of fact and gossip that he heard in this way, and vividly describes Huneker in *A Book of Prefaces* (New York: Knopf, 1917), *Prejudices, Third Series* (New York: Knopf, 1922), *My Life as Author and Editor* (New York: Knopf, 1993), and the preface he wrote for *Essays by James Gibbons Huneker* (New York: Scribner's, 1919).

17. "Xt." was an abbreviation for Christ. References to religion in these letters express the writers' shared skepticism. They believed that human folly can strike in the religious realm as readily as elsewhere.

18. "slackers": Goodman speaks ironically here because he sympathizes, in part, with these protesters against World War I. People were being arrested in New York for holding rallies to oppose the draft and the war. Labor unions, socialists, and anarchists led these rallies, but the press called even sincere marchers "German agents" and "bomb-throwers." In the hysteria of the time the protesters were lucky to escape with mere imprisonment or deportation.

19. "To-Morrow": Several socialist magazines had this title.

Philip Goodman, complete with spats, poses for a French
sidewalk photographer. Mencken accompanied Goodman on
European excursions to the sources of wisdom and good beer.
(Courtesy Ruth Goodman Goetz.)

nephew of Dr. Skodolow. He will take his case to the United States Supreme Court and prove something or other by the Bill of Rights. J. Leon Berkovitz has been retained as counsel. Berkovitz has been practicing over nine years and has never had a plaintiff's case. You recollect his work in *The People v. Kaplan, Feingold, Radtkin, et al.* (121 New York), in which he artfully succeeded in excluding the bomb testimony. It was a magnificent effort calling forth praises from such men of the bar as Morris Slutkin, Benno Feldenheim and Marks J. Belber.[20]

Goodman

Dear Mencken:

Hanauer & Geldgrieben,[21] at one time the largest manufacturers of Sausage Casings in America, made an assignment this week. Leon P. Hagedorn is named as Receiver. It will be shown that their three most important customers, Sigmund Steindl & Sons of St. Louis, Schwartzenhuber & Blau of Cincinnati, and the Philip Achweighardt Co. of your city, boycotted them because of alleged affiliations with the German Government. True or untrue, the accusations became known throughout the Trade with the result that on Monday of this week an involuntary bankruptcy petition was filed against them. The

---

20. Goodman loved the vibrant ethnic stew, heavily seasoned with Jewish immigrants, that made up the socialist movement. New York has seen nothing like it since. The case of *People v. Kaplan* is imaginary.

21. Geldgrieben: Goodman has chosen a humorous name—Geldgrieben in Yiddish suggests money-grubber. The correspondents liked to apply "speaking names" to their characters—the names tell the story—so that we get a hint of the essence of Geldgrieben before we actually meet him.

house enjoyed its greatest glory in the early nineties. Hanauer, who lived near Mannheim, rarely came to this country. He took a third wife when he was past seventy. Geldgrieben was the actual head. He made large donations to Dr. Eisner's church. In fact, it was he who made possible the building of their present magnificent edifice. He died suddenly of heart failure at a Massage Establishment in Basel. There was some ugly gossip at the time.

Goodman

Jan 25, 1918

Dear Goodman:

This morning I met old Mrs. Haas on the street, and she gave me some good stuff for the *Bilder aus Schöner Zeit.*[22] Mrs. Haas is of literary stock. Her late brother, Rudolph Schnur, was for many years Eastern District reporter for *Der Deutsche Correspondent,*[23] and I well remember the singing of the *Literarische Gesangverein*[24] at the celebration in honor of his twenty-fifth anniversary as a man of letters. The ceremonies were held at

22. *Bilder aus Schöner Zeit*: Pictures of a beautiful time. Mencken collected such vignettes of a gracious past in *Prejudices: Fourth Series,* 297–99. Examples of the vignettes: "Michelob on warm Summer evenings, with the crowd singing 'Throw out the Lifeline!' . . . The long-tailed clams and Spring onions at Rogers', with Pilsner to wash them down. . . . The very dark Kulmbacher at the Pabst place in 125th street in the last days of civilization."

23. *Der Deutsche Correspondent:* Well-known German-American paper published in Baltimore from 1841 to 1918. Like other German-language papers, it was ruined by anti-German agitation during World War I. The *Correspondent* published its last issue on April 28, 1918.

24. *Literarische Gesangverein:* Literary Choral Society.

Darley Park,[25] and the oration was delivered by Pastor Sterger,[26] the well-known orator.

Mencken

Dear Mencken:

Minna Engel is here on her honeymoon. She married young Quellwasser. You remember the boy's folks. The father was the *Käsemeister*[27] in Gusdorf's delicatessen store. He had an infallible sense of weight. I have seen him measure off a pound and seven-eighths of Swiss cheese on a bet that he could come within a quarter of an ounce of the weight and bygod take the money! He was the only one in Gusdorf's employ that was permitted to go to the cash drawer and make change. Your mother will surely recollect him.

Think of that little *rutz-näse* Minna married. Many's the time I've slapped her *dokus*. (Incidentally, and in great confidence, I spent many a tumescent evening in her mam's company before she married that *aszel*, Carl Engel.)[28] She looks nothing like her mother. In fact, she's an Engel through and through. They were all dumb as gritz![29]

Goodman

25. Darley Park, a Baltimore beer garden, was frequented by German and Irish families. Later, it was developed into a neighborhood of rowhouses.

26. Rev. A. Fred Sterger of the Trinity Lutheran Church, Baltimore, an actual orator, was born in Baden, Germany, in 1856.

27. *Käsemeister:* Cheese maker.

28. *Rutz-näse:* Runny-nosed fellow. *Dokus:* German-Jewish for "backside." *Aszel:* Yiddish term for donkey.

29. "gritz": Grits, or porridge. The meaning is similar to "pudding-head."

Dear Goodman:

The news that you, too, collaborated with Frida Engel, *geb.*[30] Kirschbaum, fills me with unpleasant sentiments. I remember well how she used to assure me, that—setting aside that immoral Schneider boy, the Pastor's son—I was the only one ever admitted to favors. A man is a fool to trust a woman.[31]

    Yours, *Mencken*

[1918]

Dear Goodman:

Tillie, alas, was even fatter. She had, in fact, the largest mezzanine floor south of Newark. Once, at a picnic of the *Onkel Braesig Verein*,[32] when they were selling raffle paddles, Old Man Lothringen, being in liquor, clouted her across the dokus with one of them, and was thrown out by the committee. Tillie burst into tears—the only time I ever saw her shed them.

The literary cobbler was Hermann Weinefeldt, a Leipziger. He kept his stock of books in the back room, and did a heavy

30. *Geb.: Geboren;* that is, "born as," maiden name.

31. Mencken generally accepts the tall tales suggested by Goodman and embellishes them, as he does here. Earlier, in his reporting days, Mencken would add stretchers to his newspaper columns, not stating that they were bogus. You could believe them or not, as you chose. John W. Baer reprints some from the 1908–10 era in *Tall Tales and Hoaxes of H. L. Mencken* (Annapolis, Md.: John W. Baer, 1990). Of course, Mencken's "bathtub hoax," perpetrated in 1917, is the best known. See Robert McHugh, ed., *The Bathtub Hoax* (New York: Knopf, 1958).

32. *Onkel Braesig Verein:* The club is named for a character in Fritz Reuter's *Ut mine Stromtid,* a novel of farm life told in the Low German dialect.

trade in the little Reclam[33] editions at ten cents. He also took subscriptions for the *Gartenlaube* and *Ueber Land und Meer.*[34] He refused to handle Socialistic papers. Once, buying the books of a deceased member of the *Techniker Verein,*[35] he acquired a thumbed copy of Marx's *Das Kapital.*[36] As soon as he discovered it, he stuffed it into the kitchen stove, to the great horror of Frau Weinefeldt.

Hermann read only one author—Jean Paul.[37] He would always maintain that Jean Paul had said everything, and usually proved it. The spoofing classes used to try him with everything, from epigrams by Oscar Wilde to speeches by Grover Cleveland. Sometimes he couldn't find the passage in Jean Paul, and that, he always explained, was because his eyes were getting bad. A favorite sport was to go to him with some passage from Jean Paul, pretend that it was from Bill Nye or Robert G. Ingersoll,[38] and then watch him find it. He always fell for

33. "Reclam": Publisher known for pocket-sized popular-priced editions.

34. *Die Gartenlaube* means "garden pavilion" or "gazebo." This magazine was published in Leipzig (1853–1937). It was thought to be "cultural" and likely to improve the mind. *Ueber Land und Meer: On Land and Sea,* was a magazine published in Stuttgart (1858–1923).

35. *Techniker Verein:* Technicians Club.

36. *Das Kapital* (three volumes, 1867–95) was Karl Marx and Friedrich Engels's critique of the capitalist system.

37. Jean Paul Richter (1763–1825), German humorist and writer, started as a theology student, but soon became a writer. After fleeing creditors, he lived in poverty while producing many novels. To Mencken and Goodman he is a symbol of youthful folly—of romance, moonshine, and mush—a contrast, the correspondents maintained, to their hardheaded realism.

38. Bill Nye was Edgar Wilson Nye (1850–96), an American humorist. Nye was merely a clown compared to Mark Twain, Mencken claimed in his

the trick, and was in good humor for days. In his last years he even found cribs from Jean Paul in the Book of Genesis.

His so-called daughter, Minna, was not his daughter at all, but an orphan from the *Waisenhaus*.[39] After his death she sold all his books, married a man named Ulrich, and went to live in Roanoke, Va.

Mencken

Dear Mencken:

Right you are. Minna came from the orphanage and more than once I heard it whispered that she was the natural child of Paul Mittenhoefer. Mrs. Paul never dreamed. . . . The child was left there at the age of two by a strange woman who wore a heavy black veil. Each year on her natal day, Minna would receive a big bouquet, presumably from the woman who brought her. All this I learned from Fred Brobst, who was superintendent there for so many years. What linked Paul's name with the child was the fact that he called at the orphanage one day when she was about three years old and, slipping Fred a two-dollar bill, asked that he give her occasional attention. He never came back. Not a word of this to anyone!

Chicago Tribune column of February 8, 1925 (see *The Bathtub Hoax*, 88). But later in the same year Mencken allowed that "his comic history of the United States is full of excellent stuff" (letter to Isaac Goldberg, July 3, 1925). Robert G. Ingersoll (1833–99) was a noted American agnostic lecturer. His speeches were heretical, and thus enormously popular, and were reprinted in a series of books.

39. *Waisenhaus:* Orphanage.

It was really Dr. Ranz[40]—do you remember little Ranzie who took Dr. Schneider's place the year he made his memorable trip to the Holy Land?—who prevailed upon Weinefeldt to take in little Minna. Mama Weinefeldt was willing from the start, but Hermann always said, "What will the neighbors say?" Nevertheless, it was a splendid thing for both of them. Minna grew to be a fine girl and this Ulrich, I hear, has one of the largest barbers' supplies businesses in the South.

What a fine hypocrite Paul Mittenhoefer grew to be. Do you know that when he became President of the *Junger Maennerchor*[41] he tried to pass a rule that there was to be no liquor served until after four o'clock on Sunday afternoons? And he probably would have had it enforced had it not been for Con Rudenauer. Con at that time was pretty active in central realty and his transactions gave Paul the big bulk of his conveyancing fees. He took Paul aside one day and told him just where he stood in the matter, with the result that the county was saved!

And speaking of Rudenauer, wasn't that a queer will he left! Even though he was a bachelor he had plenty of nieces and nephews without having to leave the greater share to Mrs. Vollmer. Of course, it permitted of only one interpretation— that old Con had better taste than the world had credited him with. Poor Vollmer lived the rest of his days with shame in his heart.

Do you recall how when Dr. Schneider returned from his vacation abroad, we were filled up for months and months

40. Dr. Ranz: The pastor of the congregation is always accorded the honorific Doctor.
41. *Junger Maennerchor:* Young men's chorus.

with lectures on "Jerusalem As It Is Today," "In the Valley of the Jordan," "The Sanctity of Gethsemane," "Where Pilate Stood," "Fair Nazareth" and "From the Manger to the Cross" —with Stereopticon[42] slides?

Goodman

Dear Mencken:

Tillie lebt![43] What a wife was she! Did ever a woman mother a man as she did Uncle Fritz? Fritz, you remember, never came home for his lunches. Tillie would prepare the meal and send it down to the store in one of those old-time lunch stands containing four porcelain pots (you haven't seen one in years!) heaped heaven high with (top pot) *einlauf*[44] or *Erbsen Suppe;* (second pot) *gebratener Rinderbrust;* (third pot) boiled potatoes, kohlrabi and *breite* noodles; (fourth pot) a note to Fritz written hurriedly in pencil saying: "Fritz, don't season the kohlrabi. The soup has plenty of salt. Be home early for supper; it's Gretchen's night out."

You hit on a perfect name when you thought of "Tillie." All Tillies are good souls, unselfish and self-sustaining. When Mrs. Spaetz's little girl, Frieda, was sick, who sent over chicken broth every day but Tillie? When poor Mrs. Heimgaertner's brother came to this country from Stuttgart, who put him up, board and all, until he got his first job but Tillie?

42. Stereopticon: A double Magic Lantern, which provided a stereo image.
43. "Tillie lebt!": "Tillie is alive!"
44. *Einlauf* is egg-drop soup (chicken stock with an egg beaten in). *Erbsen Suppe* is pea soup; *gebratener Rinderbrust* is braised brisket of beef; *breite* noodles are wide noodles.

And when the Cannstatter *Volksfest*[45] took place at Handel and Haydn Park in the Spring, who was out at the *Bayrische*[46] Booth every morning cooking the sauerkraut but Tillie?

Will you ever forget the night of Sadie Staedtmuller's wedding? Sadie's papa was collector for the Rheingold Brewery, and Fritz threatened that he would go in training[47] for the event. After the ceremony at the church the whole party went over to Fred Hessenbruch's for the grand spread and lo! poor Fritz found himself placed at the table next to Dr. Schneider[48] and his wife. Of course, the dominie's glass was turned down. Tillie was never herself when the Doctor was around. She would freeze up and act like the daughter of Cotton Mather.[49] She whispered something to Fritz; Fritz frowned, but made a low reply out of the southwest corner of his mouth. Tillie gave him a sharp look and then Fritz sullenly took his glass and reversed it, too. But at Gus Schaeffer's funeral Fate dealt him a better hand. He was an honorary pall-bearer along with Louis Schmidt, Carl Rossmassler, Herman Krauter, Henry Hessermann and Max Woebke. Tillie had forewarned him not to repeat what he did at Martin Engel's funeral (your mother used to tell you about that), but to be safe she decided that she

45. *Volksfest:* Folk festival. Cannstatter Park was a private Baltimore beer garden until about 1917. Cannstatt is a northern suburb of Stuttgart.

46. *Bayrische:* Bavarian.

47. "go in training": Uncle Fritz was practicing to drink his share.

48. Dr. Schneider was the pastor, or dominie.

49. Cotton Mather (1663–1728), famous Boston clergyman and religious writer, was often considered a prig. "The Blue Laws were passed in 1723, and go back to the hell fire harangues of Cotton Mather," Mencken wrote in *The Smart Set* (May 1913): 112. Mather may have come to mind because his enormous *Diary* had been published in seven volumes in 1911–12.

would go out to the cemetery with him. At the last moment it was announced that the pall-bearers would all go in the same carriage. Well, the funeral party waited forty minutes at the cemetery for the pall-bearers' carriage to arrive, and when it did it was decided that in deference to poor Gus Schaeffer's bones the grave diggers had better carry the casket instead of the pall-bearers. Tillie was mortified, but what she said to Fritz when she got him home nobody ever knew.

I have often wondered why Fritz and Tillie never had children. Did your father ever tell you the facts in the case?

Goodman

Jan. 1918

Dear Goodman:

The family physician, Dr. Wolf Gieseke, now a venerable ancient, has told me that Aunt Tillie was incapable of procreation on account of a prolapsed uterus,[50] with attendant damage to the adjacent tubes—the result of lifting a wash-boiler full of *Kartoffelklösse* at a picnic of the *Kriegerbund* (of which her father, Uncle Ferdinand, was *Erste Schatzmeister*) at Handel and Haydn Park, in 1884.[51] The thing weighed at least 250 pounds, and as she lifted it from the greensward to the stove (helping Mrs. Tarowsky, the Bohemian charwoman), she felt

50. "prolapsed uterus": The uterus has dropped out of position. This is rarely due to anything but a difficult childbirth, which Mencken suggests happened in this case, when Aunt Tillie "was brought to bed prematurely" and suffered a miscarriage.

51. *Kartoffelklösse:* Potato dumplings. *Kriegerbund:* Veterans' society. *Erste Schatzmeister:* Chief treasurer.

something give in her interior. A bride of six months, she was brought to bed prematurely, and thereafter found herself shut off from the felicity of maternity.

But who will ever forget her devotion to the issue of her sisters, cousins, sisters-in-law, etc., etc.? There was never a lying-in that did not see her at her post, boiling the chamomile tea, laundering diapers, and pumping the new one full of sweet spirits of nitre.[52] One of her gentle offices was to burn *Wacholderbeeren*[53] on a shovel whenever the little darling (company being present) shat itself—a primeval disinfecting, characteristic of the times. Have you forgotten how she nursed her sister Wilhelmina's twins through measles, chicken pox and mumps, all in one winter? It was during that winter that Uncle Fritz, left unguarded, drank a whole *Achtel*[54] in one hour at the Bismarck *Kommers* of the *Gelehrte Liedertafel*,[55] and so used himself up that Dr. Gieseke ordered him to bed for two days.

In 1891 Tillie decided to adopt a boy, Hermann by name, from the *Allgemeine Waisenhaus*.[56] You know why she gave up the plan? Because that abhorrent scandal-monger, Cousin Nettchen Schultz, whispered to the ladies of the *Hilfsverein*[57] that the creature was the natural child of poor Fritz, by a ser-

---

52. Sweet spirits of nitre, potassium nitrate, is administered in water solution for the relief of fever through inducing perspiration and for pain relief. Because of its diuretic effect it would no longer be used for infants. A "lying-in" is confinement for childbirth.

53. *Wacholderbeeren:* Juniper berries.

54. *Achtel:* An eighth of a liter. Mencken pokes gentle fun at the imaginary Uncle Fritz, here floored by a little schnapps.

55. *Gelehrte Liedertafel:* Scholars Choral Society.

56. *Allgemeine Waisenhaus:* General Orphanage.

57. *Hilfsverein:* Medical volunteers society.

vant girl named Ottilie, who afterward married Steinfelder, driver for the Valhalla Brewery. Fritz, of course, was innocent. He swore to Tillie on his death-bed that he had never violated the vows made before Dr. Schneider, and he told the truth.

Fritz was an honest man, and as Dr. Schneider said so beautifully at his funeral, he was his own worst enemy. It was at this funeral, by the way, that the brethren of Scharnhorst[58] Lodge, No. 74, A. F. and A. M. stopped at Adam Dieterich's on their way home, and got into a lamentable row with a crowd of low Irish. Old Mr. Blankenagel, the worshipful master, carried a black eye for weeks, and was not seen at the meetings of the Johann Wolfgang Schiller *Bauverein*.[59] This Mr. Blankenagel's son, Heinrich, married an American girl, and changed his name to Henry Blank.

Mencken

Dear Mencken:

Elias Pfaelzer, founder of the Pfaelzer *Harmonie*,[60] celebrated his eighty-third birthday this week. He lives with his daughter, Mrs. Ehrlich, and in the evening just a few of the old-timers came around to wish him joy. Gunther Frankl, who is now the

58. Gerhard von Scharnhorst (1755–1813) was a Prussian general and military theorist.

59. *Bauverein:* Building and loan society. Mencken appears to be having fun with the name. Both Friedrich Schiller and Wolfgang Mozart originally had the first name Johann. Mencken combines these name fragments to create a parody of the overblown names so effectively used to lend an ersatz importance to small financial institutions.

60. *Harmonie:* Singing club. The name Pfaelzer means a person from the Palatinate in the Rhineland.

head of the *Harmonie*, wanted to open the big hall and make an affair of it, but Mrs. Ehrlich thought it best not to, in light of the fact that the old man has had a pretty bad winter, what with a touch of pneumonia around the holidays and a serious fall in front of his own door in November. But nonetheless he was in great spirits, surrounded by his five children, nineteen grandchildren and thirty-four great-grandchildren. They presented him with a mammoth floral horseshoe in the center of which was the word "Papa" and under it "83." Nothing was served.

I remained only long enough to exchange pleasantries with the old man, but in those few minutes I saw Gus Eichenlaub, who married Tillie Zorn (Tillie is at present in childbed), Julius Freytag, himself getting along in years, Adolph Laehmke and his wife, Mrs. Chris Wohl, still a widow to my great amazement in spite of her surpassing *Rinderbrust*[61] mit Kohlrabi (these pie-and-milkeries that nowadays flourish in every street are killing off all our eligible suitors), Henry M. Ellenbogen, who handles all the old man's realty matters, and Frieda Eberstadt and her mother. Frieda's marriage has been annulled. She received word week before last through Father Halle. Everyone is curious to know the details. Yet what could be plainer than the fact that young Anton was recently rejected by his Local Board?[62]

Your Buchsbaum, the caterer, awakens recollections of his memorable scrap with old Gundelfinger, the *shamus* of the

61. *Rinderbrust:* Brisket of beef.
62. "Local Board": Draft board.

Hanover Street *shul.*[63] I'll tell you the story sometime—unless you already know it.

Goodman

Feb. 4th [1918]

Dear Goodman:

That Elias Pfaelzer is still alive fills me with astonishment. It was always my impression that he had died of exposure following the funeral of old Anton Gegner, president of the Goethe and Schiller Permanent Building and Loan Association, in 1903. This funeral took place on March 1, the day of the blizzard, and the ceremony lasted three and a half hours. By the time the pallbearers of Carl Schurz[64] Lodge, No. 39, A. F. & A. M. reached Adam Dieterich's place on their way home, five of them were in a state of collapse. Luckily enough, young Dr. Fritz Spangenberg happened to be in the barroom when they arrived, refreshing himself after a difficult buttock delivery[65] in the neighborhood, and he at once administered stimulants. Three of the old men, however, had to remain at Adam's

63. *Shamus:* Caretaker for a synagogue. *Shul:* Synagogue.

64. Carl Schurz (1829–1906), Union general and friend of Gen. Franz Sigel, was a hero to German-Americans. Schurz considered the abolition of slavery to be a continuation of the social reform that he had championed in Germany prior to coming to America in 1852. He became a senator, newspaper editor, and author.

65. Mencken is referring to a breach delivery childbirth, in which the baby may come buttocks first. Such a birth is slow, and is now usually handled by Cesarean section.

overnight. Papa Pfaelzer was one of them, and I always thought that he took pneumonia and died soon after. Perhaps I confused him with old Horst Plumacher, for many years secretary of the *Kriegerbund*.[66]

News: Young Teenie Langenfelter is engaged to be married to Otto, the oldest boy of Adele Eisenbrandt, *geb*. Kraus. I think you knew Adele back in the eighties. She was the Kraus girl who played the harp.

Mencken

Dear Mencken:

Kraus? Kraus? I knew no Krauses. . . . Can it be that you mean the Krausemeyers who kept the Hand Laundry on East Baltimore Street a block away from where the Zinkhands lived? They had a son—a boy of beautiful muscle—who used to demonstrate the Whitely Exerciser in a drug store window on Calvert Street. In the summer he sold score cards at Oriole Park. But I recollect no daughter.

You did not say if you know the story of the fight between Buchsbaum and old Gundelfinger. If you do, there's no use retelling it. And if you do, it's likely that you, in your *goyish*[67] prejudice, side with Buchsbaum.

Goodman

66. *Kriegerbund:* Veterans club.
67. *Goyish:* Non-Jewish, Gentile.

February 6th [1918]

Dear Goodman:

You will get the Woman book,[68] such as it is, by March 15. I am glad of the chance to rewrite and embellish Opus XV.[69] I'll make it a really good book. Your selling plans inflame me. But a man trained under old man Bornschein in the carpet business surely ought to know how to make them buy.

A disgusting detail has been overlooked. I always put publishers in the press, and squeeze twenty-five free copies out of them, instead of the usual ten. This is my sole *ganovry*.[70] As for royalties and so on, I trust to Kent J. Goldstein, my lawyer. He can always prove that something is due me. You will become well acquainted with his young process-server, I. Mortimer Hartogensis.

Yes, I have heard the story of the Buchsbaum-Gundelfinger combat, but always from prejudiced parties. Anton Roesser, the anti-Semite, was always talking about it at the *Turnverein Vorwärts*.[71] Old Buchsbaum himself never mentioned it in my

---

68. "Woman book" refers to the manuscript of Mencken's *In Defense of Women*.

69. Based on Mencken's idiosyncratic counting system, *In Defense of Women* would be his fifteenth work. It was the second book he did for Goodman.

70. *Ganovry:* Thievery. The Hebrew word *gonif* means "thief."

71. *Turnverein Vorwärts:* This was the largest German club in Baltimore. The name *Vorwärts* ("Onward!") stressed their call for social action. The Turner Societies were a German institution for decades, the brainchild of Friedrich Jahn (1778–1852), Prussian pioneer of physical education. The failure of the 1848 revolutions in Europe sent thousands of disappointed and

hearing. I have an open mind. Let me hear the kosher version. ⸢Goodman's reply is missing from the correspondence.⸣

My congratulations. I'll probably be in New York on March 3d, and shall be present at the ringside.[72] I hope the piece is as good as "Alone in London."

Mencken

Dear Mencken:

Why have we not mentioned Charlie Grosholz's barber shop? I was reminded of it today when opposite me in the subway I beheld the living image of old Gus Schmidlapp, who used to have the second chair. Did you know that Gus had more private mugs[73] on his shelf than even Charlie himself had? I have seen of a Sunday morning during those memorable waits as many as six men pass up their turn so that Gus could 'tend them. Also did you know that the *Tonsorial Review*, issue of May 8th, 1894, gave him a writeup and among other things

---

fearful German radicals, the "Forty-eighters," to America. Turner Societies appealed to these radicals with a combination of gymnastics (*Turner* means "gymnast") for the body and liberal reform for the mind. As vocal supporters of Lincoln in 1861, Turners came under attack in Baltimore—their armory was destroyed and their newspaper ceased publication. This was a foretaste of the attacks that would face the German-Americans again in 1917.

72. "at the ringside": Mencken planned to be in the audience to watch Goodman's new play. Goodman would later produce plays, but in 1918 was only a playwright.

73. "private mugs": The personalized shaving mugs of his regular customers. Barbers figure in these letters as ideal representatives of the common man; even better, most were German at this time.

said that he was the first barber ever to use hot towels after shaving?

I used to play checkers with him on summer evenings. My God, what combinations he knew! But just the same, he saved me money once. It was the time that Charlie was interested in that Hair Restorer recipe. You recollect how he buttonholed his customers to buy stock in the company, promising 500% dividends. Well, I was about to fall for it, when Gus slipped me the dope privately that the stuff was no good. And luckily for me. Later on he sold the "secret" to some Cleveland concern for thirty-five dollars, who would get it out under the name of . . . I believe they called it Herpicide or some such name. . . . Anyway, Gus gave me the tip alright, alright and I'd play his judgment across the board anytime.

Gus once won a prize of fifteen dollars in a honing contest conducted by Adam Pfromm & Bro., the barber's supplies firm. All the other contestants honed in the old-fashioned way—that is, they used lather as a lubricant. Gus, he put a drop of St. Jacob's Oil on the stone and he won in a walk. He knew a lot of things like that. Why, it was he who cured Sig Glixmann's boils. Sig had been to one doctor after another with no results. Gus made a poultice of raw clams and inside of a week Sig was wearing starched collars again. And piles!!! He put the leeches on old man Seidenbach (and God knows if ever a man needed two *asoles* it was Seidenbach) and in ten days Seidie was *fressing*[74] himself to death once more.

Goodman

74. *Fressing:* Overeating.

Dear Goodman:

Charlie Grosholz I knew quite well. Upon the death of Jacob Wiemann, the hay and feed king, Charlie was summoned to the house of grief to depilate the corpse. He was so overcome by his sorrow that he allowed his razor to slip, and nearly cut off the defunct Jacob's nose. The slash, observed by the pallbearers of Scharnhorst Lodge, No. 74, A. F. & A. M., caused them to suspect that Jacob had met with foul play, and for a while there was a violent (though whispered) scandal, and talk of a coroner's inquest. It was hushed up by Dr. Buddenbohn, who had attended Jacob in his last moments. He actually died, as everyone knows, of *Leberkrankheit.*[75]

Gus Schmidlapp, in his old age, attained to many dignities. On his seventieth birthday the Arbeiter Liedertafel serenaded him and he was the guest of honor at a Wine *Kommers.*[76] Some time before that he had been elected Grand Archon of the German Knights of Pythias, and accorded the Grand Decoration of Chivalry by the *Hesse-Darmstädter*[77] Odd Fellows. He died worth $18,000, all of which went to his daughter Gustie, the wife of Hermann Schabernagel,[78] the hardware dealer. They have one daughter, Clara, a gifted alto; her loud, challenging voice is heard every Sunday at Martini Evangelische

75. *Leberkrankheit:* Liver disease, presumably cirrhosis.
76. Arbeiter Liedertafel: Worker's Choral Society. *Kommers:* Social meeting.
77. *Hesse-Darmstädter:* From Hesse state, Germany.
78. Schabernagel, one of the humorous German names prized by the correspondents, means "jester."

Charles Street, Baltimore, from German Street, *c.* 1890.
The Baltimore of Mencken's childhood was only a memory by the end
of World War I. Even the name German Street was deemed offensive
and changed to Redwood. (Engraving from *Illustrated Baltimore:
The Monumental City* [New York: American Publishing and
Engraving Co., 1890].)

Church.[79] As for Hermann, he is an atheist, and full of ranting against the clergy when in his cups. Gustie's money put him on his feet, and he is now said to be worth $50,000. Clara is very sniffish.

Mencken

Dear Mencken:

I was thinking the other night of the great times we used to have at the *Sängerfest*[80] in the Spring of '93. That was a carnival for you! The University of Vienna sent over a contingent that year headed by Herr Habig. I believe Kansas City won the First Award. I went every night during the two weeks. Rudolph Lipschutz was one of the ticket-takers and he used to pass me in. And on top of this I had a pull with Max Flatau, the chief usher. What has become of them? Max was quite a fellow and a flute player of no mean worth. Once when Anton Seidl's orchestra came to town, he substituted for the bass viol at a two-hour notice. The fellow's versatility surprised us all. Later Seidl sent him a letter appreciating his services. Max framed it and put it in his window where it remained for years.

He had a daughter, Hattie, who ran off with one of the Israelites, a boy named Gottlob of the rich Gottlobs. They used to tell an amusing story of the affair. Old Gottlob had publicly

79. Martini Evangelische Church: The Martini Lutheran Church was organized in Baltimore in 1867. St. Martin was an important patron saint, the source of many German names.

80. *Sängerfest:* Song contest. Singing clubs would trade visits and the National Sängerfest alternated between Philadelphia, New York, and Baltimore.

proclaimed that if any child of his ever married a *shicksa*,[81] he would disown him. When the time came to be put to the test, he found that his little Davey had gone and married the daughter of one of his best customers. Flatau threatened to throw out Gottlob's merchandise and never again buy a dollar's worth from him. Indeed, he would have held to it, too, had not Gottlob convinced him that there were *goyim and goyim*.[82]

Goodman

Feb. 19, 1918

Dear Goodman:

The greatest of all *Sängerfests* was in 1903.[83] Attendance: 27,500. My old friend, Emil Horst, had charge of the bar. This bar was a wonder. It was built in the basement of the armory and was 274 feet long. Emil employed seventy-eight bartenders, each working with both hands. Adam Scheidt, local manager for Anheuser-Busch, was personally present day and night, seeing that the malt was properly handled. It is said that he got no sleep for four days and four nights. After it was over, he was ordered by his physician, Prof. Dr. Lastner, to remain

---

81. *Shicksa:* Non-Jewish girl.

82. *Goyim:* Gentiles, as contrasted to Jews. Note the distinctly Jewish construction, "there were *goyim and goyim*." Similarly, "My son went to Harvard, and that is not just a college. There are colleges *and* colleges." The contrasting expression, when a Gentile runs exasperatingly true to form, is "What can I say? *Goyim* are *goyim*."

83. It was Baltimore's turn to host the National Sängerfest in 1903. It was a grand occasion, with Pres. Theodore Roosevelt delivering the main address.

immovable for a week. He spent the week at the shore-house of the *Unabhängige*[84] Fishing and Social Club, on Wagner's Creek, playing skat[85] with the shore-keeper, Ignaz Borstmüller.

As you will recall, the Harmonie of Union Hill, N.J.,[86] won the *Kaiserprise*[87] at this *Sängerfest*. I shall never forget the Wine *Kommers* they held that night to celebrate their victory. Gustav Schildt supplied the wine, which was mainly Erbacher 1898, with a few carboys of Bernkasteler Doktor[88] for the special guests. The speech of Prof. Ludwig Zimmermann on the origin, etiology, history, morbid anatomy and sequelae of the Seven Years' War lasted two hours, and was a titanic effort. Such days will never come again. But I have heard eloquence! And I have seen men with iron bowels!

> Yours, *Mencken*

Dear Mencken:

Why have we overlooked Harmonie Park, where Carl Woehr's Bavarian String Orchestra played nightly? Do you remember the little pink and blue drum that shielded the dozen or so mu-

---

84. *Unabhängige:* Independent.

85. Skat was a card game popular with Germans at the time.

86. Union Hill, N.J., across the Hudson River from Manhattan, is where, during Prohibition, Goodman and Mencken found good drinking. The story is told in *Heathen Days* (New York: Knopf, 1943), 202–3.

87. *Kaiserprise:* Kaiser's Prize.

88. "Erbacher . . . Bernkasteler Doktor": these are highly esteemed German white wines, the Doktor vineyard overlooking the Moselle being one of the most famous in the world.

sicians? And the gravel floor on which was laid out in careful arrangement the round iron tables and the frail iron chairs? And the Chinese lanterns that were hung on wires from tree to tree? And Joe Kunz, who ran the park, backed by George Rothfuss the brewer? And old Fritz the pretzel vender, who was half-witted or something? And Karl the waiter who handled the first seven tables to the right of the main aisle? And Frau Schauffle, who was the soloist on Saturday and Holiday nights? And Emil Ulrich, who always sat at a table near the music and talked so loud that he was a nuisance? And the beautiful Maltese cat that would often get up on the bandstand to the great amusement of the crowd? And the obnoxious Sadie Vollmer dressed in a Bavarian Alps costume, who would walk through the aisles pestering the men to purchase her made-up bouquets for their ladies? And Charlie Präger the collector for the Rheingold Brewery with his gray Fedora hat? And Mrs. Schweickhardt, Kunz's sister-in-law, who superintended the sauerkraut and *Speck?*[89] And Anton Doepel of Doepel & Ranz, the smoked beef people? And the esteemed Henry Hoerle, president of the Germania Bank? Have I forgotten anyone?

Now for some exercises in mnemonics. What was Woehr's opening selection every Saturday night? And what was his invariable finale? And what was his favorite encore? I burn to give you the answers right here, but I want to see if you really know.

89. *Speck:* Bacon, a tasty adjunct to sauerkraut.

Do you remember the familiar attitude of Frau Schauffle—the one with the palms of her hands joined together and resting coyly against the side of her face? On the difficult notes there would be just a little sway of her body from left to right. In the pause between the verses she never failed to blow her nose.

The year after Joe Kunz died the place was taken over by the Rustenbach boys, who ran it in a free and easy style. The old crowd soon disappeared. The next season the license was revoked. Then Rothfuss put Mrs. Schweickhardt's son in charge with the hope of rehabilitating the place, but it was no use—the spell had been broken. On its site today are two-story houses, and on the very spot where formerly stood the bandstand, there is a saloon kept by a fellow named Wagner.

Did you know that it was at Harmonie Park that George Rothfuss first met Lotta Altmaier? Little did Lotta dream when she went there night upon night with her folks that she would ever cover her nest so well. And old Chris Widmaier—wasn't he the proud one when the engagement was announced? Never having possessed the proverbial pot, it was the old, old story of the beggar on horseback.[90] But George was a prince of men. Indeed, he was his own worst enemy. When they sent him to Wiesbaden for his sugar,[91] I well knew

90. "the beggar on horseback": When Goodman slips into his storytelling role, he adds an imaginative twist to traditional adages. Five letters later he revisits the story of how beggars will ride. The "proverbial pot" suggests a large estate.

91. "to Wiesbaden for his sugar": Rothfuss was sent to this resort on the Rhine to treat his diabetes.

the end was not far off. Lotta's observation of his memory by never re-marrying was magnificent.

Goodman

Dear Mencken

My play went over—and lay there.[92] Their reception of it surely healed the blows of sound.[93] But Dunsany's "The Lost Silk Hat" went even worse, and "Did It Really Happen?" which, according to Nathan, is a good play met the same fate.[94] A fine bill to hand a bunch of Cloak and Suit Manufacturers.[95] Goodman, of the Washington Square Players, has taken my play for his next bill.[96]

Goodman

92. Goodman here is referring to his one-act play, "The Tongue of the World," which had been included in the Friars Club's "Second Winter Frolic" for March 3, 1918. The play contrasts outward appearance with reality; what appears to be an illicit love affair turns out to involve not one couple, but two, and a crisis for all four lovers.

93. Goodman recalls Oliver Wendell Holmes's "Old Ironsides" (1830): "And silence, like a poultice comes, and heals the blows of sound." We can appreciate that, after Goodman's play, silence was definitely not welcome.

94. "Did It Really Happen?" is a one-act play by Zoë Akins that rounded out the Friars evening, along with Swan and Mack, famous as "Two Black Crows." Lord Dunsany (1878–1957), Irish poet and dramatist, contributed to *The Smart Set*. His one-act play was on the same Friars Club bill.

95. "Cloak . . . Manufacturers": Goodman's hyperbole for an unsophisticated audience. The garment industry was dominated by immigrants.

96. The fact that Edward Goodman (1888–1962) had taken the play proved its inherent merit. Edward Goodman produced seventy plays in his career, and founded the Washington Square Players, which in 1919 became the Theatre Guild.

Dear Goodman:

Gustav Borscherding, of the family owning the lime kilns, died yesterday. He was taken off by *Leberkrankheit*,[97] the curse of the whole family. He will be buried in St. Stephen's *Friedhof*[98] tomorrow afternoon, Pastor Landauer officiating. I hear that he leaves $200,000, and that he divides it equally between his second wife, *geb.*[99] Schultz, and his daughter by his first marriage, Eva Schneidereith. They hate each other, and will lock horns over their rival displays of mourning. Eva fainted when papa died, and had to be revived by Dr. Hohenagel. When she came to she took to bawling "Papa! Papa!" so loudly that the Polizei rang the door-bell and asked if there was any need of help. Dr. Hohenagel prescribed *Kümmel*[100] in large doses, and by and by Eva fell asleep.

The widow sneered at the whole exhibition. On her part, she didn't shed a tear. When Eva hurled the fact at her, she replied that the greater grief was dry-eyed, and cited the practice of Theda Bara, Mme. Petrova,[101] etc., as proof.

Part of the women sided with her, and part took up for Eva.

97. *Leberkrankheit:* Disease of the liver, probably the result of enthusiastic consumption of alcohol.

98. *Friedhof:* Cemetery.

99. *Geb.:* Born as, maiden name.

100. *Kümmel* is caraway-seed liqueur, here an effective sedative.

101. Theda Bara (1890–1955) and Olga Petrova (1886–1977), famous actresses of silent films, may have employed a dry-eyed style, but Theda Bara, the original screen vamp, was at least known for her eyes. She employed copious eye makeup and a daunting stare. (Acting was simpler in those days.) Madame Petrova is still admired for her role in a classic, *The Vampire* (1915).

When I called, the controversy was in full blast, and so, after a glance at old Gustav in his Masonic regalia, I went down to the kitchen, and talked to Eva's husband, Hermann Schneidereith. He told me that Lawyer Buchsbaum would meet the family and explain the will immediately after the funeral. He said he had heard rumors that Buchsbaum planned to charge $1000 for his services, and that Mrs. Buchsbaum was already bragging in Hanover Market. If he does, there will be hell. Hermann says $200 would be enough. I guess that Buchsbaum gets his $1000, and a damned sight more. The lawsuit between Eva and the widow over the Bible containing the *Stammbaum*[102] will be worth at least $5000 to him, what with retainers, fees, expenses, expert witnesses, etc.

Old Borscherding was the only Suabian[103] I ever knew who was a prohibitionist. He advocated making the distilling of whiskey a felony, and would not allow the stuff in his house. Save for half a dozen bottles of beer in the evening and a bottle of Liebfraumilch on Sunday, he drank absolutely nothing. Nevertheless, *Leberkrankheit* finished him, as it finished Field Marshall von Moltke.[104] In his last days he was delirious, and sang old songs at the top of his voice. The Kesslers, who live

102. *Stammbaum:* The family tree.

103. A Suabian was a German from Swabia, an area that includes parts of present-day Germany (Baden-Württemberg and Bavaria) and Switzerland. The Suabians were predominantly Catholic, and it would be unusual for them to object to wine, a part of the sacrament.

104. Helmuth Carl Bernhard, Count von Moltke (1800–1891), the Prussian field marshal, was still healthy in his ninety-first year, and indeed up to his final hour, when he died of a heart attack. Mencken has embellished the story with a suggestion that the field marshal was too much in his cups, but we should never take a *Leberkrankheit* story too seriously. Liebfraumilch is Rhine wine.

next door and dislike the Borscherdings, rapped on the wall twice during the last night. It seems to me that this was carrying animosity too far.

Yours, *Mencken*

My dear Mencken:

Borscherding's death is a matter of indifference to me; but I am surprised to learn that Dr. Landauer has consented to officiate. You know that he refused to marry Borscherding and Bertha Schultz six years ago for very good reasons. So did Dr. Schneider for that matter. To marry a man whose first wife had been lowered into her grave but ten days before would have been to strike at basic morality and common decency. As Dr. Landauer himself put it at the time: "It would have been participating in a debauch in the presence of Almighty God." So Gustav and Bertha went before Mayor Preston. . . .

Your credulity is pitiable! Borscherding leaving $200,000. Can you not see that Melvin Buchsbaum has spread this report for his own aggrandizement? If he leaves $50,000 it will surprise me greatly. My judgment in these matters is better than yours. So slip it to Hermann Schneidereith quietly not to build his hopes too high, also that Eva will require eyes in the back of her head if Buchsbaum is to be one of the executors.

I never knew that Gustav was a Suabian. If he was, the old trickster deserves credit for one thing: he got *verstandt*[105] long before he reached forty.

Goodman

105. *Verstandt:* Good sense.

Dear Goodman:

You are quite wrong about the Borscherding estate. I have it from Hermann Klauenberg, who is secretary and treasurer of the August Bebel[106] Permanent Building and Loan Association, that old Gustav had no less than $38,000 out at interest with the association, perhaps the largest single deposit since Anton Pfinsterling quarreled with the Franconia outfit, pulled out his $55,000, and damn near bankrupted it. So much for cash. In real property, Gustav owned the family lime kiln in fee simple (say $10,000 at a forced sale), the ground under the Knoop coalyard (say $18,000), thirty-five two-story houses occupied by workmen at the Schwalbach piano factory (say $35,000), a feed warehouse in Washington, a farm in An-n'ran'cl[107] County, and a piece of land near Metz. Also, he had $72,000 worth of bonds, and owned stock in the B. & O. Railroad, the National Lime and Cement Co., and the Anaconda mine. Figure it out for yourself. Schneidereith makes it $200,000, and adds *am mindestens.*[108]

Buchsbaum tells me that if Eva Schneidereith doesn't let him administer the estate, he will file a claim for $15,000 for legal services extending over ten years. He says old Borscher-

---

106. August Bebel was a German socialist (1840–1913). Socialists are generally mentioned in these letters to poke fun at mankind's credulous nature, but the Forty-eighters who came to Baltimore in large numbers would have considered Bebel an inspiration.

107. "Ann'ran'el" helpfully provides the pronunciation of Anne Arundel County, Md.

108. *Am mindestens:* At least. More properly simply "mindestens."

ding used to back him into a corner at the *Harmonie*,[109] buy him a glass of beer, and then put a lot of hypothetical legal questions to him, thus: "Suppose A has a contract with B to deliver 400 loads of No. 2 shell lime during a certain week, at so much a load, and B neglects to provide a place to dump the lime, and A's drivers have to haul it back to the yard, and on the way home a storm comes up, and rain falls on the lime, and damages it 35% net; what is B liable for?" Gustav always pretended that he merely asked these questions to test Buchsbaum's knowledge of the law, but Buchsbaum argues that they were actually efforts to get advice out of him for nothing. He has a complete record of them, with his answers, and says he can go into court, have Gustav's books produced, and show that every question corresponded to a real transaction.

I suspect that Eva is a bit scared by his talk, and will let him have the $5000. His wife is already bawling for $7,500, and says she wouldn't live in the house he wants to buy with the $5,000. It has no stationary washtubs in the basement, the tiles in the bathroom run only half way up the wall, and so on. Moreover, it is near the Zeller bristle factory, and on hot summer nights the whole neighborhood is bathed in a sickening odor.[110] But Buchsbaum is standing firm. Even if he gets $7,500, he says, he will sink no more than $5,000 in a house. The rest he wants to invest in a gravel company that Max

109. *Harmonie:* The German music club.

110. Mencken recalled the experience from his childhood. He describes the effect of a hair factory in *Happy Days:* "When a breeze from the southwest, bouncing its way over the Wilkins factory, reached Hollins street the effect was almost that of poison gas" (70).

Dieffenbach is organizing. Max offers him a one-fourth share for $2,500, and a guarantee of $300 a year as counsel, besides dividends of at least 25%. The gravel is really there: I have seen it. Max always carries a pocketful of it, and every evening, along about ten o'clock, he drops into Karl Knortz's saloon and passes samples around. His wife you may remember. She was the Kirschbaum's Teenie—a fattish girl with very black eyes. She is active in the *Damenverein* of Fourteen Holy Martyrs Church.[111]

The Pretzfelders I remember only dimly. Ernie's uncle, Rudolph, was a baker, and hanged himself in his bakehouse, as bakers always do. The family is from Chemnitz.[112] There was another uncle, Leopold, who made a lot of money in the junk business. It was common rumor that he was a fence for a gang of lead-pipe thieves. In 1889 he was actually arrested on the charge, but it so happened that old Wilhelm Klein was foreman of the grand jury at the time, and he fixed the thing up. Wilhelm, of course, would take nothing for himself, but he made Leopold cough up $2000 for the German Orphan Asylum. In 1897 Leopold sold out to the trust—there was then actually a junk trust—and went to Chemnitz to spend his declining years. But he quarreled with all the Pretzfelder connections there, and finally had a fist fight with his cousin's husband, Kurt Lachner. Kurt got the worst of it and complained to the Polizei, who invited Leopold to remove himself

111. *Damenverein:* The German women's club. Fourteen Holy Martyrs, or *Vierzehn Heiligen,* is a time-honored name, and there is a Lithuanian church of this name on Hollins Street.
112. The city Chemnitz is a textile and chemical center in Saxony.

from their jurisdiction. He then removed to Dettingen, and at last accounts was in a hospital there, suffering from gallstones. He must be about seventy by now. His wife was a widow, Frau von Kubitz, relict of a German army captain who was cashiered for some obscure breach of the code of honor, and who afterward killed himself by jumping in front of a *D-Zug*[113] at Hanover. Frau von Kubitz, before her marriage to Leopold, used to claim that she was the illegitimate daughter of a *Hoheit*,[114] by a French governess, but Leopold made her shut off this gabble. I doubt the story. She looked far more like the perfectly legitimate daughter of a brewmaster.

Mencken

Dear Mencken:

I showed Martin Fichholtz your letter and he said you were talking through your hat with regard to Borscherding's estate. However, I wouldn't argue further with you. You're always taken in by what others tell you. Even Martin said that your credulity will cost you a pretty penny some day. All I tell you is to keep away from that *Lump*[115] Buchsbaum.

It is amusing to read of Mrs. Buchsbaum's aspirations. My God, when I look back and see her as one of those *rutznasiche*[116] Nebenzahl children living in a little hovel in Pratt Street—in those days if the children got a bowl of soup-meat

---

113. *D-Zug: Durch-Zug*, or "express train."
114. *Hoheit*: Prince or duke.
115. *Lump*: Scoundrel.
116. *Rutz-nasiche*: Snotty-nosed.

on Sundays they'd count it as a feast—and then read that nothing but a full tiled bathroom will now satisfy her, I can only repeat Schiller's famous words: "A beggar on horse-back gathers no moss."

I suppose you know that her father *selig*[117] was an old clo's peddler. Of course, to listen to her anyone would believe that he was a merchant tailor. And what a *gonif!!*[118] While you were upstairs fetching out some discarded things to sell him, he had already stripped the hat-rack in the hall of a couple of derby hats and a few silk umbrellas. There were eleven children. The one that Buchsbaum married was pox-marked. Her first name was Fannie. I believe he got $1500 with her. Ugh! They are the amoeba of society!

I hear that poor old Emil Wunderlich has to be wheeled around in a chair. There's a man for whom I have genuine sympathy. He hasn't a soul in the world. What a fellow he was in his day! He led the march the night of my first *Maennerchor*[119] Ball. I shall never forget how he came up to me, an utter stranger, and said, "Well, young man, are you having a good time?" To me he was the great Emil Wunderlich. I tried to carry myself as he did. I aped his style of dress. I even brushed my hair in his pompadour fashion. To be like Emil Wunderlich was my life-mission. And this God of my youth is now a helpless cripple. Poor Emil!

By the way, I hear that Leo G. Hochschild was turned down in the Harmonie. Can it be that the same old animosity against our

117. *Selig:* Of blessed memory. *Selig* follows the name.
118. *Gonif:* Thief (Hebrew).
119. *Maennerchor:* Men's chorus, an important German society.

people[120] still prevails? Julian Gansmeyer who proposed him threatens to resign, along with Benno Kleintisch, Jake Raab and Hermann Rothgeb. Fancy the Harmonie without these spirits.

Goodman

Dear Mencken

Enclosed please find ten tickets at Two Dollars each for Martin Quellwasser's Benefit on April 18th. The performance will be *Der Freischutz*.[121] Lester Gretz,[122] who is arranging the affair, would like to know the present addresses of Emil Neufeld, Bernard Englander and Henry Schuldiener.[123] All three were good friends of Martin in the old days and should toe the scratch in his hour of need. If you can possibly get rid of more tickets will you communicate with Gretz? Sig Schoenagel and Jake Kuemmerle thought that April 18th would be too late, but the only other open date that could be obtained was for March 27th when "Nathan the Wise"[124] is billed. Of course that was out of the question. As Charlie Grosholz put it, "You can't sell fifty tickets for that show, Quellwasser or no Quellwasser."

And another thing: Dr. Reislinger promises to have Martin in good shape by that time. He has had a terrible winter with

120. Animosity against our people: Anti-Semitism.
121. *Der Freischutz: The Sharpshooter*, an opera by Karl Maria von Weber, who was lauded by Richard Wagner as the most German of all composers.
122. Gretz: A *gretzer* in German Jewish is a constant complainer.
123. A *schuldiener* is the head janitor at a school; *Quellwasser* is spring water.
124. *Nathan the Wise* is a verse play (1779) by G. E. Lessing that enjoyed a long-lasting popularity. Jewish characters are central and the play promotes religious tolerance.

his varicose veins and attendant dilatations. He is able to get around with the aid of crutches but looks nothing like his old self. He hasn't a soul in the world except his sister, a Mrs. Kaltenbach of Chambersburg, Pa. Efforts are being made to bring her on for the occasion, but from a letter Chris Biederbeck received from her recently it is doubtful if she will come. She explains—and very sensibly, too—that to make the journey would involve an expenditure for a new black satin dress, to say nothing of railroad and hotel costs. She is not in a position to bear this expense at the present time and to take it from the Benefit Fund is to give Martin just so much less. We put it up to Martin, however, and he agreed with her, adding that she didn't have to stick her nose into every trick.

Judging by the whole-souled way in which all of us are working, the affair is sure to be a great success. We all want to hand over to the poor fellow as much as possible. Eddie Reigelmann, Martin's best friend, is doing the secretarial work—that is, addressing envelopes—and charges only 90¢ an hour for his time. He says that he would willingly do it gratis if it were not that he can work only on his "off evenings" and his eyes have been going back on him lately.

In remitting for your tickets will you be sure to add the war-tax? Also do not mind the fact that $1.50 is stamped on them. I am assured by Gretz, who is an old hand in getting up such affairs, that they are Two Dollar tickets, but that because they are for charitable purposes it looks better if an advance is given—or some such explanation. I didn't quite understand it, but it's all right.

Goodman

My dear Mencken:

Do you recollect the old aunt who used to live with the Unterkirchers? Of course you do. They used to tell everybody
that she was a Countess. Well, alas, she is dead. And what will
surprise you is the news that she was a sure enough Countess
after all. Last night, her grandniece, Kaethe Falk, took me
over some old scrap books in which was a church notice dated
September 20th, 1844, announcing—as Kaethe put it, *proving*
—that Aranka Arndt-Foerster, the aunt's maiden name, was
wedded by due process of "civil and canonical law" to Count
Julius von Walden. I am really stirred. To think that I have
spoken to a real countess! But I always knew she was above the
common herd, in spite of what you used to say to discredit her.
It only shows you that you don't know a real lady, you don't.

And so old Aunt 'Ranka was the Countess Aranka! That
means that Oskar and Richard and Marie and Herta, in fact,
all the Unterkirchers, as well as the Schuetz and the Schlegel
families with whom they intermarried, are of prime blood!
Fancy that! Can you ever forgive yourself for behaving so out-
rageously to them?

The Countess leaves no estate. Her husband's property was
confiscated in the revolution of '48.[125] Of a long and proud
line, Count Julius made no effort to rebuild his fortune. He
died in Johannesbad in 1859 of a broken heart, it is said. The
widow remained true to her troth for a half-century lacking a
few months. How beautiful!

---

125. Revolution of '48: 1848 was a year of unrest in Europe.

Dr. Eckenbein, who will officiate at the funeral, has been given all the data concerning her life, as he intends to dwell at length upon it in his address. It will be worth going miles to hear. Frieda Falk is going to take it down in shorthand, and will transcribe a few copies of it for those who cannot be present.

I have nothing further to say except that the Gretz fellow tells me you have not remitted for the tickets for the Quellwasser benefit, and that now it is too late to return them. He says that there was a carefully worded paragraph hidden away in the body of his letter which binds the recipient in the amount if the tickets are not returned before March 20th. With a confidential wink, he explained to me that he did not mail them till noon of March 21st. Gretz, by the way, is a cousin of Lawyer Buchsbaum.

Goodman

Apr. 1st [1918]

Dear Goodman:

With all possible respect, countess your ass! I have myself seen that ancient newspaper clipping, and suspect that it was concocted by Emil Oberholzer, for forty-two years city editor of the Scranton *Volksfreund.*[126] Such forgeries are easy to procure. The truth is that *Tante* 'Ranka was the daughter of a respectable *Baumeister*[127] in Erfurt, and that her late husband, Julius, was a horse dealer. He got the nickname of *"der Graf"*[128]

126. *Volksfreund:* Friend of the people.
127. *Tante:* aunt. *Baumeister:* Builder, contractor.
128. *der Graf:* The Count.

on account of his huge moustaches and high bearing, and it stuck to him until his death in 1860, not 1859. He came to his death, not by a mule-kick, nor by any other professional mishap, but by choking on a herring bone while in liquor. Sober, he might have been able to cough it out, but with four bottles of Erbacher[129] under his belt (it was his birthday) he fell short of the supreme effort, and so, after three hours of labor over him, the late Dr. Foerster pronounced him dead.

Imagine a real count having his estates confiscated as the result of a revolution. Do you fancy that the Bavarian nobility are revolutionists?[130] An idea! Look through the *Uradel Taschenbuch*[131] until your eyes pop, and you will find no mention of any Graf von Walden. There is a Graf von Waldendorf, true enough, and a Freiherr von Walden-Steinberg, but these are different families, well known to this day. I blush for your credulity. All Kaethe Falk has to do is to roll her eyes at you and sit a bit close, and you are ready to believe anything. Observe this: old *Tante* 'Ranka never once claimed personally that she was a countess. She knew that her relatives were making

---

129. Erbacher: An esteemed Rhine wine.

130. Bavaria survived the revolt of 1848 with minimal change, except for one incident that illuminates human folly. Bavaria's King Louis I was having a scandalously extravagant affair with the famous adventuress Lola Montez. With her beauty, charm, and brains, she conquered Louis and virtually ruled Bavaria by 1847. This was too much for a Catholic country; the next year she was banished, and Louis was forced to abdicate. Politics in Bavaria continued to interest Mencken, and he tells the story of the short-lived Communist revolt in Bavaria following World War I in his *Thirty-five Years of Newspaper Work* (Baltimore: Johns Hopkins University Press, 1994), 108.

131. *Uradel Taschenbuch:* Book of the noble lineage.

capital out of the fiction, and so she made no public denial, but neither did she ever support it.

She was an honest woman, and sat under Dr. Eckenbein,[132] and his predecessor, Dr. Zeller, for fifty years.

Where in hell are my books?[133]

Mencken

Dear Mencken:

Your revelations startle me. But the letter came too late. I had already sent flowers amounting to $6.50. I hate to be hoaxed.

That *momzer*[134] Gretz is now bedeviling me for those benefit tickets. He claims that, inasmuch as they were forwarded to you through me and by reason of the fact that you live outside of the jurisdiction of this state, I can be held for them. Now, for pity's sake don't leave me in the clutches of this rascal. I have visions of writs and costs. He might add a schedule of expenses into the bargain. It's not beyond him.

Now, Mencken, I must ask you to eliminate the name of Kaethe Falk from your letters. I am quite in earnest about this. She means more to me than you know.

Goodman

132. Dr. Eckenbein was the pastor of her church.

133. "my books": Mencken was waiting for the first copies of *Damn! A Book of Calumny.*

134. *Momzer:* Yiddish for "bastard." "One who, after working the salesman to death, decides to buy in a store down the block," according to David Geller, quoted by Mencken in *The American Language,* 4th ed. (New York: Knopf, 1936), 218.

Dear Goodman:

I hope you have not gone far with Kaethe—that is, not too far to get out. It is an unpleasant subject, but perhaps I should tell you—but let my brother Emil[135] do it at first hand. You will believe him, and HE KNOWS.

Tell Gretz to go to hell. You deserve his persecutions for being polite to him. The fellow is a *shnorrer*[136] of the worst sort. I remember well how he used to beg the heels of *Blutwursts*[137] in Belair Market,[138] alleging that he was out of work. Apply your hoof to the seat of his pantaloons the next time he calls. If he blusters and talks of the law, simply mention the name of Kunigunde Loringhoven, *geb.* Schmidt. You will see him blanch and sneak away. His offenses against that poor girl would make you weep. He lives in deadly fear that her brother-in-law, Franz Loringhoven, will get sober some day and make him a black eye.

One copy of the *Damn* is here, but not the others. It looks very good.

Yours in Xt., *Mencken*

135. Emil is fictitious. We recall that Mencken's father so persistently claimed to have a brother named Fred that people in Baltimore did not realize that it was a hoax. See Isaac Goldberg, *The Man Mencken* (New York: Simon and Schuster, 1925), 60.

136. *Shnorrer* is Yiddish for a beggar.

137. *Blutwursts:* Blood sausages.

138. Belair Market: One of the small neighborhood markets, a notable part of Baltimore life.

Dear Mencken:

I shall say nothing about your hand in "Moral,"[139] except to old Heinrich Dortmunder, whose pride in you knows no bounds. He, you will remember, cut your first long trousers when he was Assistant Headcutter for Gschlacht,[140] who, in those days, kept shop not far from you. Gschlacht was last heard of in Regensburg[141] where he was married again—an heiress, so Heinrich says—and came into some very fine wooded estates, his entire time being given over to their management. Heinrich had a photograph from him a few years ago showing him dressed in a hunting suit surrounded by a pack of hounds, a gun thrown over his shoulder and a Batschari cigarette[142] between his fingers. What luck some people fall into! I never cared much for him, but he certainly turned out a nice brown Cheviot[143] for eighteen dollars. Heinrich still suffers

---

139. *Moral* is a play by the German humorist Ludwig Thoma (1867–1921). Mencken and Nathan attempted an American version of the play, but it was not produced. Isaac Goldberg states in *The Man Mencken* (215) that no leading man could be induced to undertake the key role as a hypocritical moral crusader who was secretly the "protector of a highly fashionable bordello." As an exposure of pompous moralists, the play presaged Mencken's concerns of the 1920s.

140. Goodman may have chosen the name *Gschlacht* because of its resemblance to Yiddish *shlak*, which has come into English as "schlock," suggesting shoddy merchandise.

141. Regensburg: An industrial center in Bavaria.

142. Batschari: A well-known European brand of cigarettes.

143. "Cheviot" refers to a suit made from Cheviot wool fabric from England.

from the hernia caused by slipping on the snowy sidewalk in front of Hohenadel's saloon that night in July.

Henceforth your annual contribution will not be made out to the Plattdeutscher Unterstützungs-Verein, but to the Pershing Sick Benefit Society.[144] Connie Vortschluff, for twenty-six years its Recording Secretary, advised me today of the proposed change in name. May it continue its glorious work! Do you remember how it provided a life annuity to the widow and children of Val Fenstermacher? That Lawyer Buttonweisser had to carry the case through two appeals to the Supreme Court of the State of Maryland for Val's family before the money was awarded should not be weighed against it. Vortschluff explains that there would have been no litigation had not "a pretty point of law been at issue." "As further proof that the Verein wanted no advantage in the matter," says Connie, "it employed Senator Raynor at a cost of $5000 to prepare the brief."

Goodman

Dear Goodman:

My clothes were never made by Adam Pschnorr,[145] but always by the Bentz brothers, Gustav and Hermann. Perhaps you re-

---

144. This story is a humorous echo of World War I folly. German-American clubs actually had to stop supporting German charities, but here a name change would suffice. Plattdeutscher Unterstützungs-Verein is Lowland German Relief Society, and Pershing is, of course, John Joseph Pershing (1860–1948), commander of American forces.

145. "Pschnorr" reminds us of "shnorrer," Yiddish for "beggar."

member their cutting-room, with the walls covered with picture postcards, all dealing with booze. They had every booze card ever printed in the world. I once sent them seventy-five in one package from Munich. They never used Cheviots,[146] but only German cloths made in Chemnitz. When the blockade cut off the supply, they shut up shop, and are now running a saloon. Gustav has grown very fat: he would make eighteen to twenty George Nathans.

Cantor Yekele Schoengebirge, of the Congregation Mohoshef, has volunteered as an instructor in choral singing, and has been assigned to the Fourth Regiment of Zionist Volunteers, now recruiting at the corner of Baltimore and Eden Streets. Capt. Irving Inesteen (*geb.* Einstein), who is an atheist, ordered him to cut off his beard and spitlocks, but he carried the matter to Jacob Schiff, and still has them.

[Hermann Bauernschmidt has come under suspicion here after ordering Pumpernickel rolls in the Savoy Café. You may recall the combination Continental Laundry and Livery Stable he maintained in East Baltimore Street.][147] Every collar he sent home had a thumb mark on it, and at least once a month he mixed my undershirts with those of Hugh Wolfenbuttel, who then weighed 360 pounds, though diabetes has since pulled him down to 195. Hugh often says facetiously, sitting in Old Man Dingendein's place, that he has pissed more than 160

146. Cheviots come from England or Scotland; Mencken wants to switch to a German fabric.

147. The beginning of this paragraph is missing; this is a suggestion of what the original would have contained.

pounds of sugar, and that if he had it now he would be raided for hoarding.

Mencken

Dear Mencken:

When your letter arrived I showed it to Arno Hochstaeter, who was in the office at the time. He said that when he was in the laundry business in Baltimore he had more goddam trouble with you than with any other customer on his books. There was never a week, he avers, that you didn't make some sort of claim. If it was not three collars missing, it was a shirt ruined in the ironing. Luckily for Arno, one of his best customers was Otto Mastbaum, whose linen was the same size as yours. Whenever you would squeal he would dip into Otto's bundle. Once Otto complained that he was being systematically robbed, but Arno had him just where he wanted him, as his laundry was not being delivered to his right home, but to an extra-marital establishment. Mastbaum died in the Schwartzwald[148] in 1906.

You will be surprised to learn that Wolff Kriegsmann has been committed to Dr. Rieger's Private Sanitarium. It has shocked us all. Wolff has led a stainless life if ever a man did. Lena Albers, his sister-in-law, tells me in the strictest confidence that it is paresis.[149] But I cannot believe it. I crossed with Wolff in 1907 and met him again in Wiesbaden. One night I had two women at the Hotel Rose and asked him if he cared to fill in. He blushed like a young girl, admitting to me

148. Schwartzwald is the Black Forest of Germany.
149. Paresis: A general weakness. Goodman is talking about syphilis. The terminal stage of syphilis is debilitation, often termed paresis.

then that he had never been with a woman. He always expressed great friendliness for you.[150]

Goodman

May 1st [1918]

Dear Goodman

Let me know of your arrival ahead of time and I'll meet you at the station.[151] I am sick at the moment, but will be all right again in a couple of days. I dessay it is *Leberkrankheit.* My uncle Wolf[152] died of it.

Sadie's sufferings are due almost entirely, I believe, to Emil's colossal development and rough technic. I well remember how, in his single days, he was looked on with terror in certain semi-public circles. Many a time he had to pay one dollar extra to be accommodated.

Mencken

[May 1918]

Dear Goodman:

Print the libidinous manuscript, get yourself comstocked,[153] and you are a made man. Incidentally, where are the proofs of the Woman book? I have not seen none so far.

---

150. Goodman's recurring joke is to have a dubious character express a liking for Mencken.

151. Goodman was invited to join Mencken's Saturday night music group occasionally, and this is probably the reason for his trip to Baltimore.

152. Uncle Wolf is imaginary.

153. "comstocked": Anthony Comstock (1844–1915), the officious protector of morals in New York, has become a verb. Mencken suggests that suppression of the book will ensure its success.

Let Kurt Bradtmeier keep his tongue off the subject of Moselle. Does he think the clergy and laity have forgotten the time he was taken by the customs men for smuggling five bottles of Affenthaler[154] from the Norddeutscher Lloyd *Schnellpostdampfer* Dessauer[155] back in 1894? It cost his father-in-law, Emil Schandt, at least $700 to get him off. You may recall the scandal that followed the case. The wine disappeared during the trial; all the trace it left was some sinister hiccoughing among the jurymen. The foreman was Bruno Lilienthal, the *Wurst* butcher,[156] and it is generally believed that he got $100. They acquitted Kurt on the ground that there was no evidence that he knew what was in the bottles.

Karl Doppelgänger has been interned[157] for arguing (in Bopp's Maritime Exchange and Café) that there is more nourishment in a quart of sauerkraut than in four eggs. He left for Georgia[158] wearing two iron rings and his badge as chairman of the refreshment committee at the Cannstatter *Volksfest*,[159] 1913.

154. Affenthaler is a German wine. Moselle is the famous white-wine region.

155. Norddeutscher Lloyd was a large German passenger line. The *Schnellpostdampfer* Dessauer was a luxury steamship named for Dessau, the manufacturing center.

156. A *Wurst* butcher specialized in pork and sausages.

157. To be interned meant to be jailed for violation of the World War I sedition law. Mencken and Goodman felt that war hysteria was resulting in an unjust campaign against German-Americans. "Doppelgänger," meaning a look-alike or double, was chosen as an interesting name.

158. "Georgia" apparently refers to Fort Oglethorpe, an Army base where federal prisoners were held.

159. A *Volksfest* is a folk festival. Cannstatter Park was a Baltimore beer garden.

Wolfgang Anhalter has been taken in adultery with Louisa Schneider, *geb.* Sitzer, and old Schneider has retained Lawyer Baumgartner to sue for divorce. The history of this case proves that, with reasonable discretion, extra-legal carnality is almost safe. The talk is that Wolfgang and Louisa have been at it for no less than seventeen years. Until last Tuesday old Schneider never suspected.

Mencken

Dear Mencken:

The news of old Schneider's trouble in this stage of his life is indeed distressing. That it had been going on for seventeen years is too incredible to believe. Why, when I think of it, it is not more than six or seven years ago that Willy Anhalter wore deep mourning for that Mannheimer girl with whom he went steadily for so long and who died suddenly of a mysterious operation for "appendicitis."[160] But then Louisa Sitzer always had advanced ideas. I once heard her say to Dr. Benno Grieb that half the married women in the world believed in polyandry and the other half practiced it.

Say nothing of the St. Paul incident. The Pfaffenbachers are in a state of distraction. Emil's wife was the sole support of the old folks. Gus Himmelhoefer, the superintendent of the machine shop in Brooklyn where he worked, says that he was last seen Tuesday morning. The time-clock shows no noon hour

---

160. "Appendicitis" here is actually the result of a pregnancy. An induced abortion may have caused infection and, without antibiotics, death. Alternatively, it could have been a tubal pregnancy, leading to a hemorrhage and, in a day when transfusions were not common, death.

record of his number. The wife's condition is pitiable. Between sobs she confided to us that he had been receiving letters in lavender-scented envelopes recently, postmarked Buffalo. Could it be the Schiller woman? You know her whereabouts better than I.

Martin Oestreicher is going to marry again. He celebrated his sixty-ninth birthday in February last. But, as he explained to me, all his children are now married off, so why shouldn't he? A Mrs. Schultheis is to be the happy woman. You know her people. They were the Goetzes who got in that trouble some years ago for renting their properties to Painted Women for unmentionable purposes. Martin says for nine straight years they netted over 18% on their investment. The luck of some folks!

Goodman

Dear Mencken:

Kurt Bradtmeier disclaims most emphatically that he ever had trouble with the customs authorities, and says that your malevolence is your grandfather all over again. True, he was for many years engaged in wine handling, but the only thing he got from Europe was the labels—the wine came from California.

Goodman

Dear Mencken:

You will be glad to hear of Gus Klopstuck's good fortune. The lease of the Commercial House of Hagerstown has been offered to him. Although the building was erected in 1868 the house, you will remember, was completely refurnished in 1893. Gus takes over a $3000 stock of liquors, assumes a $36,000 mortgage on the furniture, linens and silverware, signs a new lease for twenty-one years and guarantees the Rheingold Brewery 1250 barrels per annum. All he is required to lay down is $10,000 in cash, the balance in notes in the amount of $22,000 covering the good will and name. The notes very fortunately are made out to cover a period of three years and only have to have two more endorsements besides Gus's. Leopold Geiger, his aged father-in-law, and Martin Wirtschneider, his wife's uncle, will go on back of them. Naturally Gus is very anxious to know what you think of it, but being a poor hand at letter-writing asked me to tell you of the good news. He is greatly exercised over this chance of a lifetime, as he puts it, and promises to write you all the details the first chance he gets. He wants to send out a little booklet or something and asked me if I thought you would write it, being as you know the Rheingold brew so well. You did as much, he said, for Louis Gindele when he opened his place in Canton.

Since writing the above I was speaking to Julius Klugmann over the phone. Julius says that in 1904 there was a foreclosure sale of the Commercial's furniture, linens, and silverware at which but one bid of $500 was recorded. In compliance with the law as regards one bid, the goods had to be withdrawn and were subsequently sold to the present mortgagor at a price said to be $375. Can it be that Gus has been hasty in his appraisal?

Goodman

Dear Goodman:

Telegraph to Gus Klopstuck at once to sign no papers until he hears from me. The Commercial Hotel is a famous lemon. The actual owner is Rudolf Schlummerbaum, vice-president of the Rheingold Brewery—a shark if there ever was one. The place is not worth seven dollars on the hoof. The drummers[161] of nine states know it as the home of the largest, fastest, wildest roaches in America. If a drummer ever stops there it is only to beat his firm out of the difference between the two-dollar rate and the three-dollar rate of the Hotel Washington. That is, he writes his letters from the Washington and charges up room and lodging there, but actually sleeps and eats at the Commercial.

I surely hope Old Man Wirtschneider has not signed his name to those notes. He is worth only $17,000 and the money represents the hard savings of forty-two years. I well remember how he used to slave away in his harness shop. He carried a sideline of canary birds, and in 1884 put out the once-famous Bismarck Canary Gravel.[162] He bought it of Hermann Schleunes, the hay, feed, cement, brick, sand, plaster and lathing man, for eight cents a bucket, and sold it for 10 cents a pound. This trade netted him as much as $400 a year, all of which went into the Dessauer[163] Building Association. His wife, *geb.*

161. "Drummers": Salesmen.

162. Canary grit is needed by many birds to grind food in the gizzard.

163. Dessau is a city in central Germany that became known for building, but not building societies. It was the seat of Bauhaus design.

Tschudi, was a famous *Sauerbraten* cook, and always officiated at the annual Wine *Kommers* of the Metzger *Liedertafel*.[164] She died in 1901.

That Beffel job will make you sweat. But I think the idea is excellent. I always find it easier to write a book by first trying out the stuff in a newspaper. One can slap down anything, and then observe the effect. It is really a capital plan.

> Yours, *Mencken*

Dear Goodman:

Max Klingbaum, whose uncle, Ferdinand Batz, drove a wagon for your father in 1879, is in jail charged with espionage. He had an old bandana handkerchief showing the portrait of Bismarck, and last Monday his wife, *geb.* Elsa Haberstadt, washed it and hung it on the line. An hour later the catchpolls[165] arrived, and now Max is incommunicado. Lawyer Eugen Kalbbrust has made gallant efforts to raise his bail, which is fixed at $100,000, but in vain. Elsa is naturally much excited, and Dr. Lindauer had to be called in last night to quiet her. She is expecting her eighth, of which, so far as is yet known, six are boys and one a girl.

Wolff Kriegsmann acquired his present affliction while serving in the Navy. I need say no more.

> *Mencken*

---

164. *Liedertafel:* Choral society.
165. Catchpolls: Police.

Dear Mencken:

Klopstuck's affairs are now in the hands of Lawyer Buchholtz, which means more *tsuris*[166] ahead, for Buchholtz is the son-in-law of old Christian Zupp, who has sold the Rheingold Brewery their malt for twenty-five years and more. Buchholtz is going over all the papers in the case, but told Gus that he would be unable to advise him as to procedure until next Monday. Zupp, by the way, has been in Baltimore for the past two weeks and will not get home until Sunday night.

Conrad Borchardt is mysteriously interested in this Commercial deal. I cannot get to the bottom of it. It seems that he was the lessee of record during the past year and upon his sworn statement as to the amount of business done, Gus agreed to take over the place. Gus now claims that Borchardt never went near Hagerstown the whole of the year except once when he had to sign a tax paper in person before the local collector. Is this Borchardt the same whose sister married young Schlummerbaum?

With regard to our Uncle Fritz, who died of Dr. Bright's ailment[167] in 1899, do you remember the dark blue double-breasted pea jacket he wore? True, he was a *Schuft*,[168] but what nonsense is this about his attending Ingersoll's lectures?[169] He

---

166. *Tsuris:* Troubles.

167. Bright's ailment: Kidney infection.

168. *Schuft:* Scoundrel.

169. Ingersoll's lectures: Robert G. Ingersoll (1833–99) was a charismatic orator who drew the largest audiences of his day. He won fame with his speech supporting James G. Blaine at the 1876 Republican national convention. "He raised an awful rumpus," recalled James Huneker, of Ingersol's Freethought lectures (Huneker, *Steeplejack*, 1:95).

went to the Second Lutheran Church in Hanover Street and was a particular friend of the Rev. Dr. Schneider. Schneider, you will recall, was a little fellow with a screechy voice and gold spectacles. I shall never forget the virtuous white lawn[170] tie he always wore. Our Aunt Tillie continually nagged Fritz by saying with a sigh, "If you were *only* as neat as Dr. Schneider!" Tillie crept on your nerves because of her persistency in prefacing every third sentence by the words, "As Dr. Schneider said last Sunday." Dr. Schneider officiated at Fritz's funeral. The oration lasted fifty-five minutes, containing poesies from his favorite author, none other than Jean Paul Richter,[171] such as, "The human countenance smiles on those that smile and sympathizes with those that weep." Aunt Tillie speaks of Dr. Schneider's tribute even unto this day, although Dr. Schneider, himself, has since been taken from his flock. "Ah, yes," reflects Tillie, "that's the way things go."

It's a lie . . . Batz never drove for my father. He never even had his hand on an inch of our harness. If Mose Fox were alive he could prove it. Batz was secretly in the employ of Dr. Krautenbein, the veterinarian. It all came out in the trial. Batz did right in turning state's evidence. In no other way could the testimony of those three witnesses have been sustained. What is more, even if it had been established that Old Geldgrieben's

---

170. Lawn: Sheer linen or cotton, notably used for Anglican bishops' sleeves.

171. Jean Paul Richter (1763–1825), a German novelist, appealed to romantics. Mencken chose a Richter quote to introduce Section VII of his book of epigrams, *A Little Book in C Major:* "A variety of nothing is more pleasing than a monotony of something."

mare had been given Paris Green,[172] only Batz's admission on redirect examination could have possibly fastened the guilt on Krautenbein. Even Lawyer Schnabel[173] admitted that before he died. Yes, sir . . . Batz did the right thing. It is not generally known that after Krautenbein finished his term, he moved to Buffalo, where he became a Christian Science healer.[174]

Goodman

May 14th [1918]

Dear Goodman:

Where are the Woman proofs? Also, did you get the contract?[175]

The Congregation B'nai Jeshurun is not alone in its sorrow. Eighteen members of the *Hesse-Darmstädter Gesangverein*,[176] serving in a certain line regiment, went over the top at St. Souville,[177] and have not been heard of since. Curiously

---

172. "Paris Green": Not only the color of the *American Mercury* cover, but a bright green powder, prepared from arsenic acid and copper acetate, used as an insecticide.

173. "Lawyer Schnabel": The name means "snout" or "talkative person," an apt choice here.

174. "Christian Science healer": Krautenbein is not only given a humorous name (literally "cabbage-leg"), he continues as a comic character, embracing Christian Science, one of the heresies that Goodman and Mencken thought illustrated the American susceptibility to quacks.

175. "Woman proofs . . . contract": Refers to *In Defense of Women*, which Mencken was completing for Goodman.

176. *Gesangverein:* Choral society.

177. "St. Souville" apparently refers to a fort near Verdun. Note the pro-German view of the war, as Mencken suggests that German-American sol-

enough, the Germans did not fire at them. Nevertheless, they did not return as expected. There is great grief.

Ah, that *Wiener Palatschinken!*[178]

Mencken

Dear Mencken:

Young Theodore Eisner, who knows my views on this subject and who hopes for the Republican nomination for Congress from this district, promises me that it will be the first business to receive his attention should he be favored with a sufficient plurality. Eisner, by the way, is the son of the late Max Eisner and nephew of *Geheimrat* Eisner of Bischofswerda.[179] Not yet twenty-four, he has given great promise as an orator and in his two or three years at the bar has made an enviable reputation. It is said—at least by his mother—that he inherits the talents of his distinguished uncle. You probably knew the sister, Lotta, who married (and subsequently divorced) the spurious "Count" von Gretz-Strelow. The affair caused no little excitement about eight or nine years ago. The "Count"—whose real name was Paul Schworst, the son of a poor but worthy tailor of Buffalo—finally drifted to Europe and when last heard of was an attendant at one of the Casino Baths at Marienbad.

---

diers are defecting to the German side. Far from defecting, the troops were actually ready to fight and in this month launched their first offensive in the war. Within six months they were victorious.

178. *Wiener Palatschinken* are distinctive Viennese dessert pancakes, apparently enjoyed by Mencken and Goodman on Mencken's last trip to New York.

179. Bischofswerda is a town in Saxony. A *Geheimrat* is a privy councillor.

That the incident killed Old Man Eisner there is no longer any doubt.

Goodman

May 16 [1918]

Dear Goodman:

Theodore Eisner has no more chance of going to Congress than I have.

If he doesn't make his wife stop playing *"Die Wachtparad"*[180] on the Pianola he will land in Fort Oglethorpe[181] instead. Why he ever married her I don't know—probably Mamma Eichhorn managed it. She is a mere light head—thinks of nothing but moving-pictures, clothes, etc.—actually reads the *Parisienne.*[182]

Mencken

180. *"Die Wachtparad":* The changing of the guard. *Die Wachtparad Kommt!* is a short piece by Richard Eilenberg. The Pianola is a brand of player piano.

181. Fort Oglethorpe, Georgia, is an Army camp mentioned in these letters as the destination of people convicted under the Espionage Act of 1917. This law was used to prosecute "sedition," which was usually no more than vocal opposition to the draft or the war. The most famous dissenter was labor leader Eugene V. Debs, who was sentenced to ten years in prison for no greater crime than stating his pacifist position. Running for president from his prison cell in 1920, he still received almost a million votes. His sentence was commuted in 1921, as the nation redressed wartime injustices.

182. Mencken, with George Jean Nathan, started the *Parisienne Monthly Magazine* in 1915 to capitalize on the pro-French feelings of the time. Although Mencken had a low opinion of its readers, it was soon making more money than *The Smart Set.*

Dear Goodman:

You will be amazed to hear that Wolf Ortman, the brewer, is talking of abandoning brewing to turn his brewery into an oleomargarine plant. He says that prohibition is surely coming, and that he wants to take time by the foreskin.[183] His belief is that the war will make butter very scarce and expensive, and that oleo will thus come into fashion. Immediately the war is over, he proposes to sell out his oleo plant to some trust or other, and retire to his estate near Augsburg, and raise grapes.

Wolf's brewery is small, and seldom heard of, but I am told that he has made $25,000 a year out of it, and is worth $300,000. He employs no *Todsäufer*,[184] but does all his soliciting and collecting himself. He brews a very bad pale beer, and has to drink it himself all day, getting around among the trade. You should see him blow off a collar of foam. Four-fifths of the beer goes into the bar gutter with it. Then, by a clever trick, he stoops and starts to drink on the way up. The saloonkeeper thus thinks that he has drunk the whole of it. He tells me that he figures on getting down about a third of it—or, say, fifteen glasses net a day.

His medical adviser, Dr. Himmelmann, tells him that this

183. The maxim is "take time by the forelock." Mencken's joke is a standard bit of naughty banter. See *Intimate Letters of James Gibbons Huneker* (New York: Boni and Liveright, 1924), 249.

184. *Todsäufer* was a brewer's agent. Etymology of the word suggests part of the *Todsäufer*'s job, which was to attend funerals and raise toasts to the departed.

will not hurt him, but that the full forty-five glasses would finish his kidneys in two years. Dr. Himmelmann makes such estimates very accurately. He can examine a man, test his urine, have him jump over a stool, and then tell him to a gill how much he may safely drink. By this means he prolonged the life of Old Man Darsch for years. Darsch used to drink thirty glasses a day and was getting yellowish and feeble. Dr. Himmelmann took him in hand, cut him down to twelve, gave him a pill or two, and restored him to complete health.

Mencken

Dear Mencken:

The Berghoffs received word this week that their uncle, Max Einhorn, died on January 20th at his place in Bieberich near Frankfurt a. M.[185] in his eighty-second year. Now what will become of the inheritance they have been anticipating these twenty years and more? Even in normal times probate would be tedious and costly. What with the war and the fact that Frau Gansz, his nurse, has claimed to be his common-law wife, I see little indeed for the nieces and nephews in this country. His estate will foot up.[186] When Einhorn and Steglich liquidated in 1894 he was reputed to be worth close to $400,000. The following year he went back to his native town. He revisited the Berghoffs in 1902 and at a family reunion intimated that some day Frieda and Paul and Elsa and Anton and Karl

185. "Frankfurt a. M.": Frankfurt am Main is a major city on the Main River.

186. "foot up": Total a considerable amount.

and little Greta (then a mere child) would some day, as the children of his only sister, enjoy the fruits of his fortune. Hugo Koch, who was then courting Frieda, was present at the time and could testify to this, but of course I do not know the attitude of the German courts with regard to the verbal testimony of an interested witness.

It is said that Einhorn met the Gansz woman at Wiesbaden, where she was employed as a masseuse. Every afternoon he would drive out to the Casino to meet her and before long she was a permanent figure in his own household. In May, when the season was at its height, they would take a suite of rooms at the Hotel Rose, closing their nearby home. Charles Wohlgemuth and his wife, who are very good friends of the Berghoffs, met Einhorn in Wiesbaden some five or six years ago. He introduced the consort as *"Frau Einhorn."* That would certainly be bad for the Berghoff claims if it ever came out in the contest of the will.

Then, too, there's another angle. While known to the world as a bachelor, it was common knowledge that he had a child with ———— ————. I refrain from mentioning the name inasmuch as the child, now a successful merchant in your city, adopted his mother's name. I have even heard the Berghoffs refer to the child as "Cousin ————." Are you familiar with the circumstance?

Since writing the above, Karl Berghoff ran in for a little call. He tells me that they have been advised through the American Consulate at Berne that by the terms of the will drawn fifteen minutes before his death, Max leaves everything to the "widow" and her two children by two former alliances.

What is all this about Wiemann being the hay and feed

king? I have it from Mose Fox's own lips that he never did over 22,000 bushels a year in his palmiest days. And Mose certainly knew—he bought enough of the stuff when he kept his livery stable. The real king was Waldemar Furst of W. Furst & Bro. It was said that their output was as high as 70,000 bushels in one year. Do you remember the old place? And do you remember the night of the fire? I watched it from across the street with Franz Klopstuck, their bookkeeper. I shall never forget when the walls fell in! It was a dreadful sight! I had to take Franz around the corner to Hohenadel's. The Lanahans got richer[187] that night. Mamma Hohenadel got out of her bed and made soup for the firemen. Chief Hogan was there at the time and I heard him say it was one of the worst fires he had ever handled. Along about one o'clock the Christian Webber Paper Box Factory, which adjoined Furst's, started too.

Nor shall I ever forget old Webber giving directions to the firemen.

Gottsferdamters[188] filled the air. Finally two cops had to drag him away. They took him to Hohenadel's. When he got there, Jake led him into the back parlor and sprawled him on the sofa. All he had on under his overcoat was his night-shirt tucked into his pants. How he escaped his death of cold that night is a mystery.

The fire ruined Furst completely. The insurance had run out two days before and Franz had neglected to renew it. The

187. "Lanahans got richer": People drank a lot of whiskey. Wm. Lanahan & Son of Baltimore were distillers of the traditional Maryland rye whiskey.

188. *Gottsferdamters:* Goddams. *Verdammters* are curses.

last I heard of Franz was that he was President of the Business Efficiency Corporation of Buffalo, N. Y.

Goodman

[1918]

Dear Goodman:

The Einhorn case fills me with sour sentiments. The old *Schuft*, by his disgusting carnality, has broken up three homes. His sister, old Frau Berghoff, has taken to her bed, and Dr. Giegnauth tells me that she is in a critical state. She is, in fact, in a delirium, and talks of nothing save that unspeakable hussy Gansz. Then there are Hugo Koch and Frieda. They have had five children in view of their expectation, and now they have nothing save Hugo's salary as head bookkeeper for Knefely, the German produce man, whose business, as you may imagine, is already shot to pieces by the war.[189]

Finally, there is little Elsa Berghoff, just married to Anton Pulvermacher, conductor of the *Harmonie*.[190] Anton, of course, loves her, but he is a man of sense, and would not have gone before Pastor Borst with her if there had not been some promise of assistance in the exchequer. He gets but $1,000 a year from the *Harmonie*, and makes but $800 more from his pupils. It was his hope (and Elsa's) that he would be able to give up conducting and teaching on Uncle Max's death, and devote himself to composing. Now his symphony in *Es-dur*,[191]

189. "shot to pieces by the war": The result of bias against Germans.

190. *Harmonie:* Choral society. In addition to this fictional group, Harmonie was the name of one of the four large choral societies in Baltimore.

191. *Es-dur:* E-flat major.

already sketched out, has gone to pot. The man's grief is pathetic. I say nothing of the other Berghoffs, or of Papa Berghoff. Paul is doing well in the lime and cement business, Anton has diabetes and can't last two years, and Karl is somewhere in Australia, and hasn't been heard of since 1914.

Moreover, Anton married Tillie Hempel, and her three children are thus taken care of by the Hempel money, made in the cigar business. Paul is a bachelor, and Karl's wife, *geb.* Schluderberg, is childless and a slut. It was because of her carrying on with an Italian, in fact, that Karl took to the antipodes. The Italian has now deserted her, and it is common talk that she receives assistance from a wealthy *Bauverein*[192] magnate. I refrain from mentioning his name.

> *Mencken*

August 6 [1918]

Dear Goodman:

Rudolph Fink the younger has been expelled from the *Hesse-Darmstädter Gesangverein*[193] for arguing that Bismarck was a greater man than Rutherford B. Hayes.

> *Mencken*

Dear Mencken:

Mamma Ehrenbacher invited me to supper Friday night. She had *Hühnerkrautbrühe*[194] made expressly for me. She said that

192. *Bauverein:* Building society.
193. *Gesangverein:* Choral society. Darmstadt is a commercial center in Hesse state.
194. *Hühnerkrautbrühe:* Chicken broth with cabbage.

she never saw anyone enjoy it as much as I did since her husband *selig* died. The old lady is greatly worried. Young Fritz is letting the business go to hell. He claims that there is nothing in cooperage any more. But Mamma whispered to me afterward that it isn't Fritz's fault as much as it is his wife's. She has high-flown ideas. She wants Fritz to go into Real Estate and Conveyancing, and always sets up Hugo Balsinger as an example. A fine example, that *Schuft!* He couldn't even keep up his poor old father's lodge dues. Mamma and I played Solo Sixty[195] and between tricks I got all the news. Hermann Lahm, who went with Tillie Barthmeyer for so many years finally threw her over and married Stella Fischer—of the rich Fischerlers—and is now in business for himself in Hagerstown; Henry Wunderlich was cut off without a dollar by his father because he married that O'Brien girl; Paul Ellenbogen is engaged to Gus Woernwag's widow; and Ellenbogen's half sister, Sadie Gretz, is being kept by old Loeffler, the brewer. He is actually past seventy-five. Mamma said she hasn't seen you since the night of Hattie Thiess's wedding. That must be sixteen or seventeen years ago. She had heard that you were doing well writing stories for the magazines.

[In a missing portion, Goodman describes his new play.] But if it does get a production you may rely upon it that Hertha Gritzmann will be there the opening night, although I am bound to say that she is not as literary as she was prior to her third marriage. Dr. Barthold Weser, her present husband, is President of the American Association of Graduate Chiropodists. He has treated our family for years.

195. Solo Sixty: A card game, a version of skat.

Karl Quellwasser and Anton Theodore Wirt are in charge of our local committee to obtain signatures on A Petition of Taxpayers to Exclude German from the Public Schools.[196] They intend also to get up a petition to change the name of the present month.

Goodman

August 15th [1918]

Dear Goodman:

I enclose a list of reviewers for the Woman book.[197] By all means send it to the women's papers listed; they will fall on it heavily, and so make a success of scandal.

Yours *in Sso. Cor de Jesu,*[198] *Mencken*

August 17 [1918]

Dear Goodman:

Please enter a subscription for the Woman book in the name of Frau Dorothea Bingel, *geb.* Schmidt, *Vorsitzerin* of the *Hilfsverein Deutschamerikanische Frauen.*[199] I have known this estimable lady for thirty-three years. She has been trying to marry me off for sixteen years. One of her earliest selections

196. "Public Schools": The study of German declined dramatically with America's entry into the war. Many school districts dropped the language altogether.

197. "Woman book": *In Defense of Women,* published by Goodman in 1918.

198. *In Sso. Cor de Jesu:* "In the most sacred heart of Jesus," a typical part of Catholic devotions.

199. *Hilfsverein Deutschamerikanische Frauen:* German-American Women's Relief Society. *Vorsitzerin:* Chairwoman.

was Wilhelmina Goerst, now the wife of Dr. Emil Hartfeldter. Her technique in those days was to tempt a young man to go too far and then appeal to his honor. I think I convinced her that this was an unsafe plea.

She now strikes directly at the stomach, and is thus more successful. I confess frankly that she almost floored me with the Widow Fink, a positive genius at *Kartoffelpfannkuchen*.[200] Well, I was lucky to escape. The Fink Cooperage Works, in which the widow had a four-fifths interest, failed a month after I got out of her clutches. She gave it out that I had made an indecent proposition to her. Nothing could be more absurd. Believe me, such an idea would scare me. The truth is that she made it herself.

I well remember Dr. Krautenbein. He used to board during the summer with the Schaumloeffels, at Ellicott City.[201] They had a hired man named Karl Krause. One day Karl was taken down with cholera morbus and the doctor dosed him with some horse medicine—about a quart. Strangely enough, it worked an immediate cure.

When do you go to Yaphank?[202]

Mencken

---

200. *Kartoffelpfannkuchen:* Potato pancakes.

201. Mencken always recalled his visits to Ellicott City, where at the age of 7 he felt "the first urge to become a journalist," Isaac Goldberg reports (*The Man Mencken*, 64).

202. Yaphank, N.Y., a town on Long Island, "was a joke—a deliciously typical joke," says Goodman's granddaughter, Judy Sanger. Mencken is suggesting that the draft is about to nab Goodman, actually a concern as the draft took older men. Ruth Goetz, Goodman's daughter, recalls that Yaphank was a "hell-hole of a camp they put all those drafted boys into." But it was not

Dear Goodman:

The incident occurred in 1899, and in the back room of Adam Potthast's *Weinhandlung*.²⁰³ Adam was famous for selling champagne at ten cents a large glass. He made it of California white wine with the aid of a bicycle pump. His boy Raymond (named after the *Raymond* overture²⁰⁴) was an adept at the process. Every afternoon at three o'clock the *Kriegerbund* used to meet in his back room to drink synthetic Affenthaler at five cents a glass. Present: old Karl Borscherding, with his wooden leg; *Lieut. d. Res.* Bruno Elberfelder; *Feldwebel*²⁰⁵ Schmidt, of the Baden Cavalry; Hugo Quandt; Max Wahlmann, who was wounded at Sedan; Hermann Brotsch; Ignatz Fink, of *Ober-Bayern*;²⁰⁶ Heinrich Wagner; and Leopold Schultz. Elberfelder was the accepted authority on grand strategy, but *Feldwebel* Schmidt was admitted to know most about the atrocities perpetrated by French *francs-tireurs*.²⁰⁷ Schultz always got drunk. At 5:30 his stepson, Wilhelm Klausmeier, then about eighteen years old, always came in to take him home. Of these old sol-

---

without its consolations. Private Irving Berlin, upon being marched out to Yaphank, wrote its first soldier-show, *Yip-Yip-Yaphank*, which introduced the immortal "Oh, How I Hate to Get Up in the Morning."

203. *Weinhandlung:* Wine store.

204. *"Raymond* overture": The opera *Raymond*, by Ambroise Thomas, is known today for its overture. The story of *Raymond* occurs again in *Heathen Days*, 203.

205. *Feldwebel:* Sergeant.

206. *Ober-Bayern:* Upper Bavaria.

207. *Francs-tireurs:* Irregular forces, guerrilla soldiers.

diers only Fink is still alive, and he is at the *Allgemeines-deutschesgreisenheim.*[208]

Mencken

Dear Mencken:

I must return for a moment to Jake Hohenadel. There was no place in all the world to match the *fresserei*[209] that Mama Hohenadel prepared. God bless her soul! When they carried her out—she had been ill for five days of pneumonia—even Karl Hoffschmidt felt a salt tear on his face. I can see her in her coffin now, lying in the parlor which was on the second floor above the saloon. There were actually twenty-three carriages. When Dr. Schneider, in his sermon at the cemetery, came to the words, "From dust thou come, to dust thou must return,"[210] poor Jake wept like a child. Fred Seiffert, Jake's bartender for fourteen years, had to put his arm around the unfortunate man's neck and beg him to bear it bravely.

Emma Hohenadel was the German interpretation of a dutiful wife—wedded to Jake for nearly twenty-eight years and twenty-seven of them spent without a corset. Occasionally she would take me back into her kitchen and give me a taste of some *Gefüllter Kohl*[211] she had made especially for Jake. Then with a wink of the eye and an affectionate slap on my face, she

---

208. *Allgemeinesdeutschesgreisenheim:* General German Old Folks' Home.
209. *Fresserei:* Feast, great abundance of food.
210. Genesis 3:19.
211. *Gefüllter Kohl:* Stuffed cabbage.

would ask me if my mother could cook so well. She really made Jake. That mortgage of $13,500 held by the Rheingold Brewery was paid off by dint of her work. I was there the day they bought the property from old Adam Kuehnle. Adam tried to saddle the conveying expenses (an old trick of his) on them, but Emma was too foxy for him. When the papers were finally signed Emma took Jake in her arms and hugged him all over. Of course, two bottles of Champagne were opened and I was in on it, but Kuehnle wouldn't wait to drink their luck, he being of the school that believes a realty transaction is one in which one of the parties is stuck. His ill temper cost him the most marvelous lunch that day, of *Ulmer Gerstl Suppe* and *Pökel Ochsenbrust* with spinach, that ever a man put past his lips.[212]

In Hohenadel's place over the center of the bar was an ambitious oil painting of Gambrinus[213] astride a beer barrel holding a *Seidel*[214] in his right arm. By his side was a female (probably Goethe's heroine,[215] judging from her long, flaxen plaits)

212. *Ulmer Gerstl Suppe:* Barley soup in the style of Ulm, in Württemberg. *Pökel Ochsenbrust:* Corned beef brisket.

213. Gambrinus is the mythical Flemish king credited with first brewing beer. Gambrinus is a common subject for paintings like the one here, celebrating the joys of beer. Mencken scholar Mayo DuBasky recalls that in Baltimore's colorful past there was "a huge wooden Gambrinus" in front of "a crumbling, dark place called Weissner's Brewery at Gay and Lombard Streets."

214. *Seidel:* Beer tankard. Mencken and his friends adopted this Bavarian term for a beer mug.

215. "Goethe's heroine": Probably Charlotte from Goethe's *Werther*. German sentimentality has produced a painting with the practical Gambrinus sitting beside Lotte, a symbol of impractical romance. Goodman rejoices in depicting these scenes of sentimental excess for Mencken's enjoyment. The fact that young people typically enjoyed *Werther* for its weepy romance, missing its

offering him another one. At his feet, manipulating the bung-hole, was a Rhenish elf drawing gleefully the amber from the keg. No one ever learned who painted it, although Jake once whispered confidentially to Hermann Hessermann that a critic once told him that it was after the best period of Oddenino, the Court Painter to Philip of Hesse. By the terms of Jake's will the painting passed into the hands of the *Junger Maennerchor*, where it may now be seen bearing the simple inscription: "Presented by Johann Jacob Christian Hohenadel, 1896."

Jake's estate was probated at $40,000. Fred Hohenadel, a son by his first wife, was cut off without a penny, but contested the will vigorously in the courts and was granted a considerable sum, how much I never learned. He was a *Schuft*[216] and came in for much notoriety during the Lottery raids. After inheriting his money, he fell in with "Al" Herford, and was really the moneyed man behind Joe Gans.[217] But after the famous frame-up with "Wilmington Jack" Daly, he had to leave town. The last I heard of him was that he kept bar at a low place in Buffalo.

Do you ever go into the Hohenadel place any more? Are the old fixtures still there? Who runs it? I shouldn't want to see it. The memories are too dear. Instinctively I would call out for

---

underlying message that the world belongs to the strong, makes the allusion that much more appealing.

216. *Schuft:* Scoundrel.

217. Joe Gans, a black boxer from Baltimore, was immensely popular as Baltimore's hometown champion. Gans was managed by Abraham Lincoln "Al" Herford, who not only promoted matches, but also served as a uniquely colorful ringside announcer. Mencken tells the story in *Heathen Days*, 96–106. It was an era of fixed fights, as we see in the next line.

some *Schwartenmagen*[218] and see before me the ghost of that sweet soul.

Goodman

Dear Goodman:

Greisenheim was not a town, my dear sir. I alluded to the *Allgemeines-Deutsches-Greisenheim*. Surely you remember the annual Greisenheim picnic, with the old folks hauled to Darley Park in phaetons.[219] The Metzger Liedertafel always used to sing, and there was usually a speech by Dr. Schneider, or by his confrere, Dr. Julius Yingling, whom he hated like poison. It was at the Greisenheim picnic in 1891 that Prof. Hugendubel, conductor of the Harmonic Society, took a drop too much, and so fell from the platform while conducting "Morgenrot,"[220] to the scandal of the veterans of the Kriegerbund. I remember his skinned nose to this day. Most of the women shrieked and ran, but old Mrs. Weissner went to the rescue, bandaged him neatly, and took him home in her dayton wagon.

Karl Hoffschmidt I never knew; our noodles always came from his competitor, Wilhelm Encke. But I hear from the venerable Mrs. Hucke, still alive at eighty-seven, that he actually went back to Bingen in 1893, and that at last accounts he was

---

218. *Schwartenmagen:* Pork head-cheese (pork snout, tongue, heart, and so on, in gelatin).

219. Phaetons: Light, four-wheeled carriages.

220. "Morgenrot": "Dawn of Day," name of an old German military song. Mencken noticed the song in Hindenburg's tomb, as he reports in *Thirty-five Years of Newspaper Work*, 312.

yet in good health. I suspect that Anna Buchholz deceived poor Karl in the matter of the herring. She prepares them to-day quite as well as her mother ever did. She actually jilted Karl. And why? Simply because Gustav Wehrle was a handsome dog, with huge yellow moustaches. He had a scar across his left cheek and talked vaguely of Heidelberg.[221] Behold the end of a romance. Gustav is now bookkeeper at the Goldbräu Brewery, and Anna takes in sewing.

Mencken

Dear Mencken:

So you know the Schluderbergs! Then you must also know the Gutschneiders from Reading. Karl Gutschneider married Minna Sachwald—one of the rich Wilkes-Barre Sachwalds. Her younger sister, Elsa, married Sigmund Schreiber of York.[222] It is through the Schreibers that I met the Schluderbergs. What a small world it is!

Charlie Schultheiss asked me if I would mention in my next letter to you that he wishes to sell his house on East Baltimore Street. Can you help find him a purchaser? He has no one left in Baltimore to look after his interests. He no longer gets about as he used to, owing to a very severe hernia. But he would take the trip down to close a deal for the property. He says there is only $1300 against it, held by the Franz Abt[223]

---

221. "scar . . . Heidelberg": Gustav wants us to think that his scar comes from romantic, dueling days as a student in Heidelberg.

222. Reading, Wilkes-Barre, and York are towns in Pennsylvania.

223. Franz Abt (1819–85), German composer, enjoyed a particular vogue in the mid-nineteenth century.

Building and Loan Assn. He would take $6,800 if the right party came along. Also there is twenty dollars in it for you, which he requested me to tell you. Charlie says you owe him this little attention for the sake of old times. He used to serve your family with milk and ice. Furthermore, he avers that your present excellent constitution is directly attributable to the fact that he never diluted the milk. Oh, yes, whatever you do, you are to say nothing to Paul Koenig, his nephew, with whom he is not on speaking terms.

Goodman

[August, 1918]

Dear Goodman:

I have put Charlie Schultheiss' house in the hands of Adolf Klauenberg, secretary of the Hesse-Darmstadt Bauverein. Adolf is a capital man for such jobs. He visits twenty-five or thirty saloons every day, and hears all the new gossip instantly. The minute an engagement is rumored, he goes to see the bridegroom-elect, rents him a house, sells him the furniture on installments, puts him up for membership in the Knights of Pythias ($500 in case of death; $15 a week in illness, up to eighty weeks), and gives him the name of Mrs. Hempel, the best midwife in town. Adolf deals in real estate, mortgages, insurance in all its forms, horses, wagons, Fords, fishing shores, pianos (including the automatic), baby carriages, home-made sauerkraut, and diamonds. His wife, Berta, *geb.* Schneider, keeps his books, and is always throwing out hints about the amount he makes. It may be true or it may be false, but this I know: that he has $8,000 drawing six percent in the Hesse-Darmstadt, and owns seven houses in a row back of Patterson Park.[224] And from what beginnings! Ten years ago Adolf was driving a wagon for Knefely, the cheese man. How he studied double-entry bookkeeping under Old Man Kurtz, cashier of the Burghardt Brewery, and became a master of Bauverein Finance—this is a story that would dim your eyes. He never takes a drink except on business, and gave up smoking a year ago. His father-in-law, Anton Stisser, opposed his marriage to Berta, but is now very proud of him.

I know of no man more useful to know. Say your roof leaks, and the tinner, collecting seventeen dollars, only makes it worse. Well, you call up Adolf, and in an hour he is on the scene with an expert roofer from Elberfeld, a man trained at the *Hochschule*[225] there. Result: you pay nine dollars, Adolf takes half—and your roof is tight. Or suppose you are giving a party, and want a reliable woman to make the *Kartoffel-klösse*,[226] wash the dishes, and otherwise help in the kitchen. Just send for Adolf, and he finds her, instructs her and guarantees her. Again, suppose you want to give your wife a diamond ring, and balk at Castleberg's prices. Well, Adolf can get the precise ring from Hugo Wattenscheidt, the wholesaler, at 35% discount. Or suppose you buy a house, and then find that the title is shady, due to the carelessness of that shyster, *Rechtsan-walt*[227] Fischer. Well, Adolf quietly unloads it for you on a

224. Patterson Park: A Baltimore park constructed in 1827 on an elevated plateau with panoramic views.

225. *Hochschule:* Institute, academy.

226. *Kartoffelklösse:* Potato dumplings.

227. *Rechtsanwalt:* Lawyer.

greenhorn who never heard of land records. Or suppose you have $1,000 loose and want to get it to work. Send for Adolf: he has mortgages on everything from a fishstand in Belair Market to the new *Gemeindehaus* of the St. Matthias[228] congregation. Altogether, a man of merit. Tell Schultheiss to be at ease. He will get his $6,800—and Adolf will get a damned sight more than twenty dollars.

I remember Charlie very well. Ask him if he recalls the way we boys used to slip bullfrogs into his milkcans while he was taking something for his dyspepsia in Freund's family liquor store.

Mencken

Dear Mencken:

Charlie will have naught of Klauenberg. He stormed when I told him what you had done. You might have known as much. Ever since that ugly affair with the *Witwe*[229] Lissauer he has proven himself to be unworthy of trust. For your pains, you are now accused of being in on the deal for all there is in it. To say the least, it makes it very embarrassing for me.

Goodman

Dear Mencken:

Paul Schnurr, who used to sell wash-wringers and carpet-sweepers in the old days, asked me for your address. He is now

228. St. Matthias: Apostle chosen by lot to fill the place of Judas Iscariot (Acts 1:23–26). *Gemeindehaus:* Meetinghouse.
229. *Witwe:* Widow.

selling insurance and wants to interest you in his new proposition, which offers with every $100 premium a choice of either two lots in Southern Alabama or a set of the Complete Works of Louisa Mühlbach.[230] He assaulted me, but, as you know, I already have property in Alabama and have read all of the Mühlbach books.

Goodman

[Aug. 1918]

Dear Goodman:

1. It was Clara ————, but I had better not tell you her last name; she is happily married. She said she had always wanted to try a literary man. She knows me from Knapp's School,[231] and would not believe that I had written a book. She said she always wondered how anyone could have patience enough to write a whole book. Her first husband was—but again I had better shut up. Suffice to say that he was a very talented man, and was always called upon to open the books of a new building association and to engross[232] the resolutions when the president of a *Liedertafel* died. He could draw the most amazing birds, each with a letter in its bill. He was run over by a

---

230. Louisa Mühlbach (1814–73) was the author of historical novels of Prussia, Austria, and France.

231. "Knapp's School": Just before his sixth birthday, Mencken was enrolled in Knapp's Institute, a private school in downtown Baltimore.

232. Engross: To write in a fair large hand (*en gros*). German-American engrossings were ornate, combining drawings with words to create memorials of births, marriages, or legal agreements. These documents are now recognized as folk art. Birds and nests were typical decorations.

train one Sunday afternoon while returning from the Western Schützen Park.[233] Clara later married Lawyer ————.

2. If Paul Schnurr asked you for my address it was a mere bluff. If he met me on the street he would leap down the nearest cellar. He will not forget the time I caught him going through my overcoat in the Garderobe of the Eintracht Gesangverein.[234]

Mencken

Dear Mencken:

Your unfortunate affair with the Winterfeldt girl has come to my ears. The uncle, Paul Suesskind, spared no details. I cannot account for your lack of delicacy. You knew, as we all did, that Lotta's share from her father was only $5,000 and not $20,000 as was first whispered. Besides, what if the principal did not pass to her until she was forty? You would have had but three years to wait. It seems to me—and I'm sure it would appeal in the same way to any outsider—that you might have found out all these matters beforehand instead of wasting the best years of the girl's life. From hints that were thrown out I do not be-

233. Schützen Park was a common name, lasting long after the vogue of shooting matches. Baltimore's Western Schützen Park was a favorite recreation ground for Mencken's family and other German-Americans. The recreation of choice was often dancing and beer-drinking, but in Mencken's day shooting clay pigeons was popular as well.

234. Eintracht Gesangverein: Harmony Choral Society, a traditional name for singing clubs.

lieve that you have heard the last of the matter. Lawyer Behrends says that the girl has not left her bed in three weeks, and that the correspondence offers certain Exhibits that no body of twelve honorable men could fail to be impressed with. I should retain Max Schuldfurth. He is excellent in such matters. But I tremble for you if you ever get on the stand and are subjected to Behrends' grilling. He is unsparing and you may be certain that he will bring up your old affair with Kathe Freihofer. May God assist you now as he did then.

Goodman

P. S. Paul Suesskind wants to know if he, as executor of the Winterfeldt Estate, were to waive that clause which relates to Lotta getting the principal when she is forty—if he could get an Order from the Surrogate to turn over to her the money at once—would you be inclined to reconsider the matter. Only Behrends' fee of $500 would have to be deducted.

Sept. 1918

Dear Goodman:

The Winterfeldt allegations give me no concern. The following stand ready to describe in exact detail the peculiar scar on Martchen's *mons Veneris:* Max Krodt, Kurt Appenrodt, Hermann Kraus, Hermann Zinkand, Theodor Ingelfritz, Johann Thierfeldter and Nikolaus Hucke. Naturally, they went further than mere looking, and will say so. Worse, I can prove that the unspeakable wench once loosed her girdle to a semi-savage, Wilhelm Cassidy, oldest boy of that Teenie Schlens who scandalized the Arions[235] back in 1885 by marrying an Irishman. I welcome my day in court. *Caveat emptor.*

Mencken

Dear Mencken:

Father Todenacher of New Elberfeldt . . . could that be the same Todenacher family that formerly lived in Lancaster? The old man was in the leaf business[236] and used to be good for an order of 25,000 Sumatra labels twice a year regularly. There were four boys. Hugo, the oldest, was found dead in a brothel; Karl had a dyeing & cleaning establishment in Buffalo when I last heard of him; Maximilian studied Law, but afterward went on the stage and one season supported Eugenie Blair; Mark, the baby, I have lost all track of. There for a while he was Society Editor on the Philadelphia *Item*.[237] The next time you see the *Pfaff*[238] ask him if he is of the same family.

Goodman

Sept. 1918

Dear Goodman:

Father Todenacher, of New Elberfeldt, is only distantly related to the Lancaster branch. The Lancastrians are bitter Protes-

---

235. The Arions: Popular name for artistic groups. This name was used by one of Baltimore's four large choral societies.

236. "leaf business": Selling tobacco, cigars.

237. The *Item* was published in Philadelphia between 1846 and 1930.

238. *Pfaff:* Priest.

tants, and never speak of his reverence, save now and then to hint that he is illegitimate. Old Franz Todenacher, the head of the Lancaster house, was a friend of my grandfather's. The two were once in partnership in the pseudo-Havana business. That is, my grandfather[239] bought empty Havana bales in Key West and Tampa, old Franz filled them with Lancaster County seed-leaf[240] made up into Havana-like hands,[241] and then the two exported them to Hamburg. Worse, they sold some of them in Key West. Those Spaniards down there have no decency. Young Maximilian (he is now fully fifty) is in the movies. Mark married the widow Blumenberg (you will remember Heinrich Blumenberg's Family Café in West Philadelphia) and is now living quietly near Red Lion, Pa.[242] He has grown very stout, and is said to have *Zuckerkrankheit.*[243]

Send me some Woman books. I want a few for gals who have been kind to me.

Mencken

239. Mencken's grandfather, Burkhardt Mencken, bought cigar tobacco in York and Lancaster Counties in Pennsylvania, and exported it to Key West. Mixed with other leaf, the tobacco would be made into cigars that would pass for Cuban. Thus there is at least some truth to this tale.

240. Seed-leaf: Broadleaf tobacco that looks like Havana leaf.

241. "Havana-like hands": After sorting, tobacco leaves are tied into "hands," bunches that have not been stripped from the stem. Thus prepared, the Pennsylvania leaf may pass as Cuban.

242. Red Lion, Pa., is Mencken's ideal of the unspoiled country town, being located in a tobacco-growing area that has retained its German customs. Later, Mencken tells the story of "A Girl from Red Lion, P.A." in *Newspaper Days.*

243. *Zuckerkrankheit:* Diabetes, the sugar disease.

Dear Mencken:

Then your grandfather must have known Saalberg Bros., who were indicted in 1892 for tampering with cigar Revenue Stamps. The Saalberg factory was in York, Pa., where they made the famous "M. S. Quay"[244] five-cents cigar, one of the biggest sellers in the East. Jakob Saalberg left the country two weeks before the trial and was last heard of in Meiningen, where his wife's folks came from. The other two brothers, Conrad and Emil, faced the music and were jointly fined $10,000. A few months later they sold their interests to a half-brother of Todenacher, one Goeckel, who ran the business into the ground. I remember clearly that Todenacher's partner—probably your grandfather—was appointed receiver and at a forced sale he sold the machinery, stock and good will of the business for less than $4,500. Todenacher accused him of rank betrayal and took the matter to the courts, claiming that a dummy purchaser had been used. What the final outcome of the case was, I do not know, as I left York about that time and moved to Columbia.[245]

Goeckel afterward went into the peat moss business, investing his few remaining dollars in a specially-prepared product that he imported from Holland. The business thrived for a time until one night his warehouse burned to the ground. His

244. Matthew Stanley Quay ("kway") (1833–1904), of Pennsylvania, makes an unlikely hero for cigar immortality. Quay was elected to the U.S. Senate, but charges of corruption prevented his reelection in 1898. In those days before the 17th Amendment, the state legislature selected senators, and though Quay was out, at least he was able to block the election of anyone else. The governor tried to appoint him senator *ad interim*, but there was a public outcry and the U.S. Senate refused to seat him.

245. York and Columbia are towns in Pennsylvania.

insurance policy had lapsed two days previous due to the negligence of his nephew Willy Bodenkampf. Goeckel committed suicide by jumping from a train near Reading, Pa. the week following. Willy collected $2000 on an old accident policy as he proved that he was Goeckel's nearest kin. I could write a history about that family. Indeed, it was the circumstance of old Franz Todenacher choking to death on a fishbone that really brought me back again into the church.

Goodman

[Sept. 7, 1918]

Dear Mencken:

As is my custom on Rosh Hashanah, I spent the day in the Synagogue. We have a very nice Orthodox Temple out here; indeed, today Selig Unverzagt, the president of the congregation presented it with a pair of solid gold scrolls for the Talmud Torah, said to surpass even the ones in Temple B'Nai Jeshurun in Buffalo. But this I doubt. The Jeshurun Talmud is mounted with over seventy carats of diamonds, and passes in enfeoffment to the first Synagogue of Zion to be built in Palestine. It was so specified in the Deed of Gift by the donor, Harris Mandelbaum.

The presentation exercises today were very simple. Just before the reading, Rabbi Nebenzahl called President Unverzagt from his pew to come upon the pulpit. There the Rabbi took the right hand of the president in his and began to slowly chant the familiar, "This is the Torah, the banner under which Israel fought for the one and eternal God." Unverzagt, head bowed, appeared to be overcome by the impressiveness of the ceremony. The slow reading to the accompaniment of Bach's *Capriccio on the Departure of a Beloved Brother* required thirty-five minutes.[246] Mrs. Unverzagt began to sob bitterly and had to be escorted from her seat. The tenseness of the moment affected every heart in the little building . . . and every eye. I doubt if any man was ever so honored before.

The ceremony over, Unverzagt stepped down and with a slight bow to the congregation said in a voice that was perceptibly affected, "Friends and fellow members of this body, I thank you from the bottom of my heart for the acceptance of my gift. However slight its importance—and it is but slight as compared to what I would wish to give you—you have received it in the spirit that it was offered. I thank you." Just that, no more. Brief and neatly turned. After the services it was announced that there would be a reception tonight in the Unverzagt home to more properly thank the distinguished man for his gift. I wish you could have been there. It would have melted even your soul.

Goodman

Sept. 9, 1918

Dear Goodman:

My private advice is that the Congregation have Louis Untermeyer[247] examine those scrolls. I well recall the experience of

246. *Capriccio on the Departure of a Beloved Brother:* A work of pathos that effectively conveys sorrow and anxiety. Goodman loves to parody melodramatic scenes.
247. Louis Untermeyer (1885–1977), poet and anthologist, was a mutual friend and a frequent contributor to *The Smart Set.*

the Congregation Oheb Shalom with the candlesticks (seven-in-one) presented to it in 1899 by Old Man Garfinkle, the carpet man. They turned out to be made of some common metal, something like solder, and began to melt during service. Garfinkle blamed it upon Fineman Brothers, who had made them, but Fineman proved by letters that they had cost but thirty-eight dollars net cash in ten days less 3%, and not $3,000 as was stated. The Garfinkle girls were greatly humiliated by the exposure, and all of them later married out of town.

Hay fever has me by the ear and ass: I am in intense discomfort, with asthma nights. If you mailed the Woman book Thursday, then Burleson has taken it home to read.

Mencken

Sept. 12 [1918]

Dear Goodman:

I am floored by hay fever. A fine asthma half of last night. Have Rabbi Fleischmann pray for me. There is no one to say Kaddish[248] should I pass away. Also, if the chance offers, please ask him confidentially if a son got by adultery is competent to do it. The matter has always worried me. The younger Holtzmann boy, Gerhard—his mother, you may recall, was the beautiful Elma Dincklemann—is the one I refer you to. Respect my confidence! He is now fifteen years old, and wants to study to be a doctor. Old Dr. Sauerwein, the family adviser, says he shows great talent. Elma tells me he is always catching

---

248. Kaddish: Jewish prayer, in this case for the dead.

cats, drowning them, and cutting them up. He also has a remarkable talent for getting out splinters and taking specks of dust from the eye.

Gerhard owes his being to his legal father's drunkenness. Shall I ever forget the day Holtzmann invited me to dinner, and then got loaded at Obst's with Benno Schwartz, Karl Lohmann and that crowd, and left Elma and me to wait for him, playing Mendelssohn duets on the old Knabe square?[249] And how dusk came down, etc., etc. Unluckily, the affair didn't last. Elma took on almost inconceivable weight after her delivery, and is now almost as stout as old Mrs. Garthe, president of the Arion Damenverein.[250] As for Holtzmann, he has been dying of Bright's for twelve years.

Yours, *Mencken*

Dear Mencken:

Rabbi Fleischmann cannot answer your question offhand. There seems to be a dissenting opinion. Maimonides[251] holds that the practice is perfectly regular, but Rabbi Hillel[252] in his great Commentary says that the Kaddish rite is reserved only for the "flower of the seed," which has always been interpreted

249. Knabe square: Knabe brand pianos were manufactured in Baltimore; the square configuration is old-fashioned.

250. Arion Damenverein: The women's club associated with the Arion choral society.

251. Maimonides (1135–1204) was a renowned organizer of Jewish law.

252. Rabbi Hillel (fl. 30 B.C.–A.D. 10), ethical leader, laid the foundation for the later study of Jewish law.

as meaning the legal offspring. If you are still perplexed, why not put the question to Al Herford?

Goodman

[Sept. 1918]

Dear Mencken:

The enclosure will undoubtedly interest you. Mrs. Egelheiser was an Adels before her marriage—a daughter of the Adels of Adels & Goerz, the wagon-builders, whose factory used to be near your former home. She had a sister Lina who married Emil Pfefferkorn. He moved to Augsburg some years ago and later received the *"Verdienstkreuz"*[253] for having invented the Mentholated Keg which keeps beer at an even temperature for periods as long as six months. Emil has grown rich. His estate at Bautzen,[254] which is open now that Fraulein Frieda goes to school at Dresden, is said to be worth more than half a million marks.[255] I have often thought that Frieda would be an excellent catch for George Nathan.

Your levity regarding our late Cardinal[256] is in very poor taste. While not a member of the Church, I am known to many good friends in it as a Reverant Recusant.[257] Thus I resent

253. *"Verdienstkreutz":* Distinguished Service Cross.

254. Bautzen is a manufacturing city near Dresden.

255. Half a million marks, at that time over $100,000, would be over $1 million today.

256. New York's John Cardinal Farley had died September 17, 1918.

257. "Reverant Recusant": An unorthodox believer who does not attend services.

your irrision. On Tuesday, God willing, I shall pay my last respects to the dear departed and at his bier shall utter for you Benediction Number 954, which begins as follows: The blind in spirit shall receive the Father's blessing, etc. etc. *Requiescat in pace.*[258]

Goodman

Dear Mencken:

You'll get a finished book next week. You are slightly ahead of Nathan in sales and leagues ahead of Hopkins.[259] We sold 1,500 copies up to the time I left the office today. That's not so bad.

By the way, I was in Ostendorff's last week and ran across old Karl Hengelmuller. You remember when Karl married Greta Einhorn. He made no secret of the fact at the time that Greta had a very rich aunt then living in Köln. Greta was the favored niece, or the only one, I forget which. Anyway the circumstance of the aunt facilitated the *schittische.*[260] What do you think happened?

The story of the aunt was a hoax all along. Karl said that he

258. *Requiescat in pace:* May he rest in peace. A visit to the library does not disclose such a benediction, but Goodman preferred his own inventions to the traditional forms.

259. "Nathan . . . Hopkins": Goodman had published books for George Jean Nathan (1882–1958), the theater reviewer for *The Smart Set,* and Arthur Hopkins (1878–1950), the Broadway producer. Here Goodman reports sales of his first book for Mencken, *Damn! A Book of Calumny,* which would have three printings in 1918. A "finished book" means Mencken will soon see a copy of *In Defense of Women.*

260. *Schittische:* Betrothal, match.

waited a year and never opened his mouth about the rich relation. Then two years passed and three and four, but never as much even as a line from Köln saying that she was sick, or that she had been sick, or that she expected to be sick. Karl one day wrote to the postmaster of Köln, his suspicions having naturally been excited, asking for the venerable woman's address. The information came back that no such name was listed in the local Kaiserliche Post's records!!! That's what I call a dirty, rotten trick, Mencken.

I asked him what his mother-in-law said when he confronted her with his discovery. Her defense was cute. "Karl," she said, weeping, "Greta liked you and I liked you, and Mrs. Ahrendts had told us how backward you were with her Hannah, so I thought it was the best thing to do." She threw her arms around his neck and they both exchanged kisses of reconciliation.

Karl and Greta have nine children.

Goodman

Oct. 2 [1918]

Dear Goodman:

The express service is hellish. The books have not yet come in. A package from *The Smart Set* has been eight days on the way.

Father Ignaz Schlumm, of the *Franziskaner*[261] Church, has left town suddenly and under mysterious circumstances. Perhaps if you will look up Joseph Hartleben, the shoe-findings[262]

---

261. *Franziskaner:* Franciscan.
262. "shoe-findings": Tools necessary to work on shoes.

man, he will be able to throw some light on it. There are all sorts of rumors. Strangely enough, he is not accused of crim. con.[263] All the gabble is to the effect that there is some trouble over those building lots on the Belair Road.[264] You will remember that the rev. gentleman bought the Schumacher[265] farm, divided it into lots, and offered them at forty-nine dollars each to Catholic families and $100 to Protestants. Now it appears that he spent the money on gorgeous banquets, given at the old Schumacher homestead to the more dissolute clergy, chiefly Polish priests from St. Wenceslaus'.[266] I hear that the chief witness before the ecclesiastical court will be Mrs. Borscherding, his housekeeper. She went to the Cardinal when a priest named Father Stanislav tried to kiss her. She is a very respectable woman.

The Sadowa Building and Loan Association is now paying 6 3/4 % on money, and could use $50,000 more, so the secretary, Ferdinand Blumfelder, tells me. If you desire to get aboard I could pass you off as a *Bayrischer*.[267]

Mencken

263. "crim. con.": Criminal conversation, which is illegal sexual intercourse.

264. Belair Road runs from downtown Baltimore through Germantown to Bel Air.

265. Schumacher: Shoemaker, another reference to shoes in this story.

266. St. Wenceslaus (1361–1419), especially loved in Poland, makes an unlikely saint. He did take an interest in Polish affairs, but was noted for drunkenness and the neglect of his duties.

267. *Bayrischer:* A Bavarian.

Dear Mencken:

Ja, six and three-quarters percent! The Sadowa people will be lucky to pay one hundred cents on the dollar at maturity if they continue to invest in those Third Mortgages in Curtis Bay.[268] Besides, Bernhard Stellgebauer is on the Investment Committee and I've had my fill of him. When Old Man Meyerlein's estate was being settled Stellgebauer was called in as a expert appraiser; there was a parcel of land near Sparrow's Point[269] which he said on oath was worth not more than $125 an acre. By a secret agreement with Leon Arnheim, Meyerlein's son-in-law and chief executor, the land was sold to a dummy. The two of them have cleaned up not less than $30,000 on the deal. Thanks just the same for the tip.

The Schlumm incident does not interest me. Anyway, how would Hartleben know anything about it? He has been on his back for sixteen months with varicose veins. Dr. Frauenthal sees him twice a week and says nothing can be done. I have been wanting him to call in Dr. Bischoff, but he refuses. Bischoff did wonders for old Mrs. Wunderlich. In fact, regardless of what the family says, it was asthma that killed her and not the veins. Even Galen[270] if he were here would displease some people.

Goodman

268. Curtis Bay: A suburb south of Baltimore. A real estate boom started here in 1878, creating a big business in arranging mortgages.

269. Sparrow's Point is on the Chesapeake Bay just east of Baltimore.

270. Galen (fl. second century A.D.) was a famous Greek physician.

Dear Mencken:

The books went off to you days ago.[271] I'm sorry if the delay has caused an alarming secretion in your testiatory glands. (In the absence of more definite knowledge I give you the benefit of the plural.) But as old Barney Feingold used to say in refusing to buy a machine for sewing buttons on garments, "It can be done by hand just as well."

Ernie Saltzmann gets married on Thursday. You remember his first wife, Teenie Baltz. The Baltz & Schweig Wagon Works used to be near your former home. Number Two is a Schlegelmilch. I hear they are well-to-do. The father was formerly in the piano case business. Do you by any chance know them?

Goodman

October 4th [1918]

Dear Goodman:

I have had Lawyer Biemueller investigate the delay in the arrival of the Woman books. He tells me that 60 express cars are tied up in the Hillen Station yards, with no one to unload them. He advises extreme caution. Every kicker is put to work by the *Polizei.*[272] His client, Irving Schapiro, of Schapiro Bros., the pants kings, is up in the air. The firm has 40,000 gross of buttons in those cars.

---

271. Goodman was sending complimentary copies of *In Defense of Women*.

272. Mencken describes the problem of moving freight at the height of the war. A "kicker"—complainer—found himself pressed into service to help with the work.

You don't say which of the Schlegelmilch girls Ernie Saltz-mann is espousing. If it is Dora, then tell him to throw in the high gear at once: she is tough. But if it is Emma, then let him remember that she had a cervix operation four years ago and cannot stand rough work. The little one, Lottie, is said to be a virgin. But I am sure she wouldn't marry Ernie. She could have had Dr. Ulmstaetter, now interned, and is very finical. Old man Schlegelmilch is worth $150,000, half made in piano cases and the rest in the Franz Sigel Bauverein.

I finished that damned *American Language*[273] book last night.

Mencken

Oct. 4th [1918]

Dear von Goodman:

Old Mrs. Pfannenbecker, who sold *Heringsalat, Kartoffelsalat, Marinierter Hering*,[274] etc., in Hollins Market for forty-three years, passed away last night. A good woman, though all of her children turned out badly. She was the oldest member of Martini *Evangelische* (orthodox) *Gemeinde*,[275] and will be

273. *The American Language*, Mencken's best-known book, was published by Alfred A. Knopf in 1919.

274. *Heringsalat:* Herring salad with such adornments as potatoes, beets, and carrots. Mencken's Saturday Night Club found herring salad restorative after a night of music. *Kartoffelsalat:* Potato salad. *Marinierter Hering:* Marinated herring.

275. *Gemeinde:* Parish. Martini was a Lutheran congregation and had both German and English language services. The "orthodox" congregation may be those who continued to attend German-speaking services.

buried in its lot at Loudon Park[276] Sunday afternoon, Pastor Julius Zeidlitz officiating. The Arion *Damenchor* will sing.

Mencken

Oct. 7th [1918]

Dear Goodman:

The thirteen books arrived today, just too late to save me $4.50. I had retained Lawyer Daniel Henninghausen to enforce my rights, and when the books came in and I called him off he insisted that he was entitled to his fee, inasmuch as he had already drawn up papers for the U. S. court and sent a boy with a summons to your Uncle Kann—twelve cents for expenses alone, what with the six cents carfare. He demanded $10.00 cash, but we compromised on $4.50. Please send me the money.

The enclosed letterhead reveals the whereabouts of Old Wolf Stiefelbaum's boy, Fritz, who had to leave New Freedom, Pa., in 1891 after the affair with the Dingledein girl. I wonder what old Wolf would say to it.

His other son, Rudolf, had a seed-case[277] factory in Lancaster County the last time I heard of him. He married a Dunkard[278]

---

276. Loudon Park: A large cemetery in western Baltimore. Mencken wrote an advertising pamphlet for Loudon Park Cemetery Company in 1902, "setting forth the comforts of eternal life in its cemetery."

277. "Seed-case" may refer to starting tobacco plants. Tobacco seeds are extremely small; starting the plants has been a challenge since the earliest days of cultivation.

278. Dunkard is a Baptist sect, noted for pacifism and plain dress. The name comes from dunking, a reference to triple-immersion baptism. They oppose the use of tobacco, so there may be an intended incongruity in a seed-case manufacturer marrying a Dunkard girl.

girl, Frieda Koontz by name, and had frequent issue. She brought him $10,000, and he joined the Dunkard communion in gratitude, but refused to leave off his collar and cut off his moustache. This caused a good deal of talk in the New Lebanon neighborhood, but it seems to have died down.

Fritz was bred as a paper-hanger, but has gone in for chattel mortgages[279] in the West. I have heard said that he has a mortgage on every piss-pot in Polk County.

Mencken

Dear Mencken:

Thanks for *kislar aga*.[280] Your erudition is almost as great as Old Matthaeus Glaenzerkopf's,[281] who came in third in the Master's Chess Tourney held in your city in 1893. If you will recollect, he was jobbed out of the first prize. Being advanced in years, his kidney and bladder became greatly aggravated just about the time of the tournament. The result was that he had to leave the room almost every quarter of an hour to *brunce*.[282] In one of these spells of absent-pee-ism, Ferdinand Fahrt moved a piece and upon resuming the game Old Matthaeus was *bekocked*[283] in five moves. He could never un-

279. Chattel mortgages are security for loans on movable, personal property, such as furniture and farm equipment.

280. *Kislar aga:* Mencken had identified this Turkish term meaning the chief eunuch, apparently in a letter that is missing from the correspondence.

281. *Glaenzerkopf:* Shiny head. Another humorous name, clearly appropriate here.

282. *Brunce:* Urinate.

283. *Bekocked:* Knocked out.

derstand that so inferior an adversary as Paul Bleimuller could have defeated him. It was the following week that he was committed to the Lutheran Home for the Aged.

Goodman

Dear Mencken:

If you can get here by Saturday evening I want you to join me in attending a banquet to be tendered to *Mohel*[284] Leventhal in honor of his having completed fifty years of professional life. Congregation B'Nai Jeshurun will be there in a body to present him with a gold lancet on which will be inscribed the figure 13,452, being the number of babies he has unerringly attended. Rabbi Grabfelder will make the presentation address and young Joel B. Hammerschlag,[285] the congregation's attorney, will speak on "The Mosaic Injunction[286] and its Relation to Modern Life." Cantor Vogelstern will render the beautiful "In Israel I Abide."

There will be a public circumcision, Marx Jacobson and his wife having agreed to lend their little baby, which was born on Monday. The ceremony will not want for sentiment in that Marx himself was attended by the venerable man. Leon Hirschbein, that *momzer*,[287] is arranging the affair and plans to bring the child to the table after the Mohel's address of thanks.

---

284. *Mohel:* Religious official who performs circumcision.

285. Hammerschlag: Hammer blow.

286. "Mosaic Injunction": "And he that is eight days old shall be circumcised" (Gen. 17:10–14).

287. *Momzer:* Bastard.

During the operation, those at the table will rise and remain standing with their glasses filled. When it is all over, Sol Koshland will propose a toast. There will be dancing later in the evening. Try to be on hand.

Ex-judge Dittenhoefer announces the engagement of his daughter Hilda to the Rev. August Meininger of South Bethlehem. Hilda, you will remember, was one of the Judge's responsibilities from an extra-marital affair. On her death-bed, his wife made him swear to her that he would take the child as his own, although for twenty years she would not permit her to darken their threshold. The mother, it is often whispered, was none other than Louisa, the rosy-cheeked Lithuanian chamber-maid at Zinkhands'. In those days, the Judge—he was a struggling law student then—and Carl Hoffschmidt shared Mama's third story back. Louisa's room adjoined. Well, a man ain't made of wood! And some, like the Judge, are made of iron.

Goodman

Oct. 10 [1918]

Dear Goodman:

Why ask me if I am willing to do a little whoring? Tell me what it is and I'll do it. If necessary, I'll do a piece proving that William G. McAdoo is the Son of God.[288]

I am sorry that I can't get to the Mohel's Jubilee on the

---

288. Mencken has been asked to do a little freelance writing. He would even go so far as to say something nice about McAdoo, Wilson's secretary of the treasury. McAdoo's name assaulted the eye daily in newspaper ads for Liberty Loan bonds.

Shabbat. Congratulate him in my name and in that of my grandfather. In his early days he did an extensive box-trade[289] as a sideline, and thus met my grandfather, who was represented by fully 200 clergymen, first and last. His most successful agent, however, was not the Mohel, but old Mr. Bacharach, collector for the Hebrew Aged People's Home. Bacharach attended all weddings, funerals, birthday parties, etc., and usually brought back orders for at least five or six boxes of Plantations. When he tackled the rich, such as Jonas Strauss and Isidore Sonneborn, he sold La Princessas, at eighteen dollars a hundred. He died in 1894.

Hilda was not the ex-judge's issue. I hear on the best authority that she was put over on him by Louisa. Her real father was Gustav Schleunes, at that time a driver for the Consumer's Ice Company, but now owner of the Enterprise Sash-Weight Works. At least, so Louisa thought herself. She was very loose, and I am told that, on rainy Sundays, with the old folks drinking coffee at the Arion's, all five of the Zinkhand boys, Emil, Charlie, John, Herman and Adolph, would enjoy her *seriatim*, in the order of seniority.

    Mencken

Dear Mencken:

I have it confidentially from Cleveland Moffett[290] that he is ready to show that the epidemic[291] was caused by the Kaiser's

---

289. Box-trade: That is, the Mohel sold boxes of cigars.
290. Cleveland Moffett (1863–1926), American writer of books and plays.
291. "epidemic": Influenza raged across the world in 1918, killing 20 million people. In the United States, at least 500,000 people died from the flu and

special agents. He says that he wrung the confession from poor old Adam Weinsturzl, one of the star loungers at Wohlfart's *Weinhandlung* on Second Avenue. Adam has been living on a small allowance from his daughter, Mrs. Meyerling, and has about ten cents a day for smoke and drink. With a dollar a day free from Moffett, he says he can now pull himself together and pour out to the great journalist the whole secret. *Everybody's*[292] has landed the story. Adam has already been photographed in a dozen poses by Arnold Genthe.[293]

Mr. Meyerling and the grandchildren are all very proud. Adam will resume his old custom of taking his Friday night dinner with them, a custom which was broken off some five or six years ago for some inexplicable reason.

Goodman

[Oct. 1918]

Dear Goodman:

I have been asked by the American Protective League,[294] on account of my skill with *Plattdeutsch*,[295] to take part in its pa-

---

its resulting bacterial pneumonia. In the hysteria of the time Germans were accused of causing the flu. In this tale, one old German turns it to his advantage.

292. *Everybody's:* A magazine published in New York from 1899 to 1929.

293. Arnold Genthe (1869–1942) was known worldwide for his portraits of presidents and other notables. He had been in exactly the right place in 1906 to record the San Francisco earthquake for posterity.

294. The American Protective League, the bane of German-Americans, was an excessively patriotic foe of the Hun, and even investigated Mencken during the war.

295. *Plattdeutsch:* The North German dialects.

triotic hunt for the perpetrators of the epidemic. Though I surely dislike to bring Emil Odenschlager to the gallows, I can't resist this appeal. Accordingly, I shall attend the oyster roast of the *Techniker Verein*[296] at Oscar Muth's shore on Sunday afternoon, and keep my ears open. Adam Weinsturzl is innocent, you may be certain. The old man was canned months ago. Moffett is being deceived, probably by that *Schuft*, ex-Lieutenant Behringer, whose false testimony jailed Hugo Horst. Behringer was expelled from Baden for picking pockets.

Mencken

Oct. 14th [1918]

Dear Goodman:

My best thanks. What with liberty loans every few weeks, soldiers' wives to assist with new (and very expensive) underwear, etc., I am so depleted financially that I welcome harlotry.[297] Would a nom de plume settle Saylor's tremors? If so, I'd actually prefer it. It would rather embarrass me at the office to sell outside what I am also doing for the *Smart Set.* Let us talk it over when I get to New York. I'll be there next week. May I victual with you Thursday, October 24th?

I hear that Knopf[298] is laid up with the influenza.

Unluckily, I can't introduce you to Teenie Schlens. Our affair is now on so sentimental a basis that bringing in a *locum*

296. *Techniker Verein:* Technicians' Club.
297. "welcome harlotry": Mencken would be glad to do some freelance writing.
298. Alfred A. Knopf (1892–1984) was about to become Mencken's exclusive publisher.

tenens[299] would affront her. But if you say so I'll put you next to Tillie Weinefeldt. Her husband, formerly bookkeeper for Fox, has gone into the horse business on his own hook, and is said to be making a lot of money dealing in cavalry remounts in Nebraska. The trade keeps him away from home, and I believe that Tillie is suffering from grass-widow's neurasthenia.[300] She is a perfect thirty-six.

I am loafing after finishing *The American Language.*

Yours, *Mencken*

Dear Mencken:

In your innocence you offer to furnish the Weinefeldt woman. Would you have me alternate with Dr. Sigismund Katz? The Doctor, with his fiery nature and ungovernable temper, would stop at nothing to defend his honor. Unless you can convince me that you are better informed on what is going on in your own town, I shall have to look to others in matters of this kind.

I might say, if I cared to carry tales, that young Berthold Freihofer could tell you a thing or two or three about La Schlens that would be disquieting to you. Understand me, I am not the one to bring up the past, but in these carryings-on with you let her not forget a little child that she put away some six or seven years ago and which, to this very day, is being supported by Berthold's mother. I always say that a man is not a man who would talk about a woman no matter how low she

299. *Locum tenens:* Substitute.

300. Grass-widow: A woman separated from her husband. Neurasthenia is neurotic depression.

has sunk, but Teenie Schlens can't put anything over on a friend of mine, no she can't!

If she denies the Freihofer affair, just ask her where she lived when she went to Philadelphia that time and how she earned her money. I'll tell you. She lived at 732 Buttonwood Street and her honest bread was bought by sitting around at nights with other girls in the big back parlor in a white Kimona. There, if you must know! Mind you, I have nothing against her, and I don't want you to think that I have nothing else to do but to go around talking about women, but what's the truth is the truth. You won't deny that.

Goodman

Oct. 27th [1918]

Dear Goodman:

The Woman book has already lost me a good friend, to wit, Mrs. Julius Holzbauer, for twenty-seven years president of the Ladies Committee of the German Orphan Asylum. I hear through agents that she is very indignant and has demanded that Pastor Ursbruch preach against me. She particularly objects to the doctrine that the domestic arts are declining. However, I am not greatly worried. Mrs. Holzbauer has regarded me as immoral for thirty-six years. In 1882, being taken to call upon her by my late great-aunt, Mrs. Erich Schoenbild, I peed myself in her parlor, thus ruining a crocheted tidy on her best sofa. I was two years and eight days of age at the time and had been drinking chamomile tea. But she has never forgiven me, and predicted so early as 1885 that I would develop into a libertine.

August Tafelmacher, past president of the *Sozialist Lieder-kranz,*[301] announces himself as a candidate for Kaiser, Wilhelm Hohenzollern having resigned,[302] subject to the Democratic primaries. He has the support of the Butchers' *Gesangverein* and the Mozart Building Association.

Mencken

Oct. 28th [1918]

Dear Goodman:

Old Mamma Bartsch, for thirty-seven years the leading gun in Heimburg Lodge,[303] No. 73, Ancient Free and Accepted Order of the Eastern Star, is receiving congratulations on the birth of her twenty-sixth grandson. A fact! Her Emil, who married Tinie Waldmeister, daughter of old Oscar, the pretzel baker, has four sons; her Robert, by his two wives, Clara Darsch and the Widow Kuntz, has six; her two daughters, Gussie and Rita, married to Johann Fink and the Irishman, John Mulcahy, respectively, have five each; her Willie, by Mariechen Schnei-der, has four; and her baby Herman, though married to Lily Rosebach so recently as the time the selective draft was first talked of, now has two. And not a daughter in the family!

Mencken

301. *Sozialist Liederkranz:* Socialist Choral Society.

302. Kaiser Wilhelm (1859–1941) abdicated the throne and fled to Holland at the end of World War I. President Wilson had made the kaiser's abdication a prerequisite for peace negotiations.

303. Heimburg Lodge: This women's organization appears to be named for W. Heimburg, the pseudonym of Bertha Behrens. Behrens wrote light novels for the magazine *Die Gartenlaube*, mentioned earlier in these letters. The correspondents liked to poke fun at the popular taste in literature.

Dear Goodman:

The paucity of reviews of the Woman book is easily explained. William Dean Howells and Dr. Henry van Dyke[304] are conspiring against it.

You will recall old Gerhardt Goertz, whose daughter Tillie married *Freiherr*[305] Wolf von Biebersthal. For many years Gerhardt has sniffed at all proletarians on account of this alliance. Well, now he gets news that the Freiherr has joined the Socialists and is a member of the Westphalian *Bolsheviki.*[306] You can imagine his humiliation. Mamma Goertz, who is less haughty, professes to be glad of it and wants to hang out the red flag, but the old man prohibits it, and has issued orders that the name of the Freiherr be never more mentioned in his presence.

The Turnverein Borussia[307] has declared for the *Bolsheviki,* and burned its fine hand-painted oil painting of Prince Henry

304. Mencken facetiously suggests that these establishment stalwarts are in league against his *In Defense of Women.* It is probable that the two had figured in irreverent conversations with Goodman. Henry van Dyke (1852–1933) wrote such things as *The Reality of Religion* and was serving at this time as a Navy chaplain. Mencken felt that William Dean Howells (1837–1920), the noted writer, had cravenly refused to come to Theodore Dreiser's defense in 1916 when other writers joined in protesting the suppression of Dreiser's *The "Genius."*

305. *Freiherr:* Baron.

306. "Westphalian *Bolsheviki*": Westphalia was a Prussian province, and the Bolsheviks were the victorious faction in the Communist upheavals of November 1917. The combination grates on the ear, rather like "Republican hippies."

307. Turnverein: Turner gymnastic and social club. Borussia: Prussia.

of Prussia.[308] Lawyer Bernmann has resigned as president, and has been succeeded by Henry Johansson, who has the second chair in Ludwig Immer's barber-shop.

A man who will eat hard-shell crabs in November will suck eggs. The thing is simply not done. As well drink *Maiwein* in January.

Mencken

[Nov. 1918]

Dear Mencken:

Thaddeus Knatschke was overcome in the crowd during Monday's great celebration[309] and is now in a precarious condition at Dr. Weixelbaum's Private Hospital. The Doctor says that the old man's great age is against his chances of recovery. The son, Thornton Knight, Jr., has not been on speaking terms with his father for some years. What was the cause of the estrangement?

The Schubert Liedertafel won first Prize for Continuous Celebration on Monday. Their score stood: began at 5:35 A.M. —disbanded at 2:30 A.M. Tuesday morning. Julius Woerz, the

308. Prince Henry of Prussia (1726–1802) was the brother of King Frederick II of Prussia, and one of the ablest generals in the Seven Years' War (1756–63), which was a milestone in the rise of Prussian power. We would not expect Prussians to embrace communism, or the baron, a landed aristocrat, to become a Bolshevik—this is a humorous concept from start to finish. This farcical echo of the revolt of the masses in Russia is made complete when the club dethrones Prince Henry and even replaces their lawyer-president with a barber.

309. "Monday's great celebration": Apparently Monday, November 11, 1918, the armistice of World War I.

President, was taken ill along about nine o'clock in the evening. His wife says that he vomited the whole night long. He made a shameful scene. And to think that his Elsa is to marry Pastor Maiszner's son! Some parents have no respect for their children.

Goodman

Dear Goodman:

My very best thanks for the picture.[310] When I get rich and build that rathskeller[311] in my cellar, I shall have it copied on a large panel.

Maybe you thought you fooled me, but I recognized the face of old man Garfinkle at once. How often I have seen him in front of a *Mass*,[312] and in that very attitude, at the annual *Kommers* of the Arbeiter Liedertafel on *Pfingst Montag*.[313] My third cousin, Fritz Deidler, was always *Vorsitzer*[314] at this *Kommers*,

310. Goodman and Mencken would send souvenirs to each other, either from their travels, especially in Europe, or from prowling in antique shops. A favorite find would be pictures of people who could well have fit into these narratives. Such a picture would immediately be dispatched in the mail with glee. These pictures were sometimes labeled with likely names and stories, or, as in this case, were sent with a challenge to identify the image. Mencken invents a likely character—Garfinkle—without hesitation.

311. Rathskeller: Bar patterned after those in German city hall cellars.

312. *Mass:* Quart beer stein.

313. *Kommers:* Social gathering. Arbeiter Liedertafel: Worker's Choral Society; one of this name was founded in Baltimore in 1883. *Pfingst Montag:* Whitmonday, the day after Pentecost, a spring holiday. The German church has adopted this pagan festival of fertility, and celebrants, whether religious or not, enjoy the chance to spend a day in the country.

314. *Vorsitzer:* Chairman.

which began at 7:00 P.M. and lasted until dawn. He conducted the proceedings, not with a gavel, but with the traditional sword, and used to bang it on the table furiously. Along about 11:00 P.M. he would begin lying about his student days in Leipzig, and tell the story of his duel with Karl Schneidereith (later *Geheimrat*[315] in Chemnitz). They were playing Beethoven's Archduke Trio, when Karl turned two pages at once, and began sawing fearful discords on his violoncello.[316] Fritz undertaking to call him a jackass, the two parted in high dudgeon. Next day, at second breakfast in Kummer's Restaurant (near the Gewandhaus[317]), Karl fixiered[318] Fritz, and so they met in the stableyard of Sumpfmeyer's *Gasthaus* beyond Gohlis.[319] Fritz had his left cheek plowed.[320] He was very proud of the wound, and rouged it on ceremonious occasions.

Fritz was a doctor by profession, but made money building two-story houses on what used to be the city dump. At the age

315. *Geheimrat*: Privy councillor

316. Violoncello: The cello.

317. The Gewandhaus is a famous concert hall in Leipzig. Leipzig has been a great center of music from Bach onward, and an important part of this has been the Gewandhaus Orchestra, now 250 years old.

318. "fixiered": Fixed his eyes upon him with a scowl.

319. Gohlis, a suburb of Leipzig, is the site of the Schiller House at 42 Mencke Strasse, where Schiller wrote the "Ode to Joy" that inspired Beethoven's Ninth Symphony. The street, named for Luder Mencken, reflects the historical importance of the Mencken family. Mencken traveled to Leipzig in 1908 to visit his ancestral home, and later told Goodman about the trip. These letters are one way the friends shared what they had seen on their trips to Europe. *Gasthaus* means an inn.

320. "cheek . . . plowed": Refers to a small cut from a duel; such a *Schnitt* was esteemed as a mark of manhood.

of fifty he married a cutie—young Adelchen Brost, aged about twenty. Adelchen was a gay one, and Fritz died with his heart and gizzard full of suspicions. Later the widow married Rudolph Oettinger, son and heir of Hermann Oettinger, the *Bauverein* magnate. She died in 1905.

Mencken

My dear Mencken:

Be assured no Garfinkle ever sat in the Arbeiter Liedertafel. Years ago I knew one who used to hang out at Seuss's on Front Street. He was a little curly-headed roach of about five feet three, was near-sighted, and wore gold-rimmed spectacles. He was the first man to introduce celluloid collars in Baltimore. He kept a little watch repairing shop in Gay Street[321] near Monument Street and came in for more prominence than he deserved when he entertained Herr Johann Most[322] on his last visit to your town. Chief Wilkie of the Federal Secret Service came over from Washington on that occasion and warned Max that his guest was not to set foot in the District.

Max resented the Chief's interference, saying that the venerable Bakounin[323] of Avenue A was to be the guest of the local Friendship Liberal League and as such demanded that his

---

321. Gay Street was once the social heart of Baltimore. By this time the residences had largely been replaced by shops, and the best jewelers were found here.

322. Johann Most, the famous German anarchist speaker, spent years touring America. Emma Goldman wrote a reminiscence of Most for the *American Mercury* (June 1926).

323. Bakounin: Mikhail Bakunin (1814–76), the Russian anarchist writer.

constitutional rights be safeguarded. The League, at that time, met in a hall in Fayette Street up three dark flights. On this particular night, Max Garfinkle introduced Herr Most, reading his speech from carefully-prepared sheets. It required fifty-five minutes to deliver.

Most emphatically, Max was not one of us, and as for the figure in the picture reminding you of him, all I can say is that had you ever known him you would know that he never drank beer. Old Suess used to import a special brand of *Schlivawitz*[324] for him, and many a night have I seen him sitting alone at the first table on the left as you entered, contemplating the Red Gospel after the Prophet Kropotkin.[325] Somewhere among my papers I have a letter from him. In it he signed himself, "Yours For The Revolution."

The only German he ever cared for was Ferdinand Lassalle.[326] Indeed he never tired of relating the famous romance. This is to his credit, for in those days Meredith's *Tragic Come-*

---

324. *Schlivawitz:* Slivovitz, a potent brandy made from plums.

325. Kropotkin: Prince Pëtr Kropotkin (1842–1921), the Russian anarchist writer.

326. Ferdinand Lassalle (1825–1864) was a German socialist who died prematurely in a duel, despite his firm stand against dueling. His ignominious fate made him an object of derision to some, veneration to others. Lassalle planned marriage to Helena, a girl of 19 (he was 38), but her father objected to the union and locked her in her room. Soon it was announced that she was to be wed to a cousin. This led to Lassalle's duel, and the tragic result became a favorite romantic tale. Lassalle was at the height of his influence at the time of his death; as a confidante of Bismarck he was seeing his progressive ideas adopted by the Prussian government. Bismarck called him "the most intelligent and charming man I ever knew." About this improbable political alliance, see Mencken's *Notes on Democracy* (New York: Knopf, 1926), 54.

dians,[327] *Evelyn Innes*[328] nor your own Huneker[329] had yet been heard of. When *Meine Beziehungen zu F. Lassalle*[330] made its appearance he had his private copy rebound in white Morocco with gold tooling and mother of pearls inlaid. After his death, it was made known that he stuck Ferdinand Busch, the book-binder, for the job in the amount of forty-seven dollars, but it didn't leak out through Busch. There was a salt for you, Ferdinand Busch! He worked at the bench right up to his seventy-third birthday. Can you see him before you now in his craft apron, with his sleeves rolled up and his beloved tooling iron

---

327. George Meredith (1828–1909) was an English novelist and poet. Sometimes criticized for affectation and naive optimism, Meredith still won Mencken's praise for his wit and joyful use of the English language. *The Tragic Comedians* (1880) retells the melodramatic love story of Lassalle.

328. *Evelyn Innes* (1898): Romantic story of an opera singer by George Moore (1852–1933). Mencken's view in *The Smart Set* was that Moore's writing showed "irresistible charm." Moore provided key insights into the fascinating world of Irish theater and literature, and influenced Goodman and Mencken in these areas.

329. James Gibbons Huneker (1860–1921), writer and music critic, strongly affected Mencken. Huneker felt that Lassalle, "the most command-ing figure in Germany," offered a more humane alternative to Marx. In *The Pathos of Distance* (New York: Scribner's, 1913) Huneker tells the story of Lassalle's romance (49–64), and in his autobiography, *Steeplejack* (2:27–30), he recounts his meeting with Helena herself. The literary figures Goodman mentions in this letter are some of the favorites in Huneker's epic storytelling; tales of European authors and musicians filled the long afternoons that Mencken and his friends spent with Huneker.

330. *Meine Beziehungen zu F. Lassalle* (*My Relations with F. Lassalle*) (Breslau, 1879) by Helena von Racowitza is described by the *Encyclopaedia Britannica* as "a very strange book." In it, Helena tells of her affair with Lassalle, which included a secret elopement prior to the fatal duel.

gripped in his hand? He learned his trade in Leipzig, but fled in '48 as did many another good man. When I think of Ferdinand Busch the thought of that Bolshevik Garfinkle sickens me.

Goodman

Dear Mencken:

I spoke of Ferdinand Busch, the bookbinder, in my last letter. Was it ever your good fortune to know him? What a gorgeous soul was he! His forehead was like Bismarck's. He owned over four thousand volumes when he died. And he knew the contents of many of them. His favorite author was Jean Paul Richter.[331] He was the proud possessor of the first editions of the *Titan* and *Flegeljahre*,[332] for which he made two sumptious bindings. I believe the two fetched six dollars when they were sold to wind up his estate. I never knew him as well as I would have liked to. Did he participate in your local German social life? I used to ask at Hohenadel's if he ever came in there, but no one even knew him by name. All I know of his private life is that he never married and lived quietly with his maiden sister. Probably some of your people knew him. Will you inquire?

Goodman

331. Jean Paul Richter (1763–1825), German novelist who appealed to the romantics of his time. Mencken and Goodman were products of a realistic age and rejected the florid passions of the older, romantic generation.

332. *Flegeljahre:* Rascal years, teenage years. This romance by Richter came out in four volumes in 1804 and 1805. *Titan* consumed six volumes between 1800 and 1803.

Dear Goodman:

My apologies for the unaccountable error. When I said Garfinkle, I meant, of course, Golinghorst. Somehow, the two names became confused in my mind. Golinghorst was of the *goyim*, and even, when in his cups, an anti-Semite. Garfinkle I remember very well. He was nearer 4 feet 3 inches than 5 feet 3. It was of him that Leon Steiner (you recall him—the wedding comedian) said that he was so short that he had to stand on a brick to spit into a duck's anus. You will be astonished to hear that his daughter Babette, who studied the violin under Prof. Josef Hennighausen, later abandoned music and married a young rabbi from Wheeling W. Va., by name Dr. Israel Goldblatt. I daresay that Dr. Goldblatt, by this time, is a bishop, or even a cardinal. He never has been heard to mention his late father-in-law.

Another famous Red of those neolithic times was Kuno Lauterdahl, Todsäufer[333] for the brewery in Butcher's Lane—I forget its name. Kuno always wore a red necktie, and used to give copies of Stirner's *Der Einzige und sein Eigenthum*[334] to sa-

333. *Todsäufer:* Brewery collector. According to Mencken (*The Smart Set* [December 1922]: 51), the brewery collector "was a man of comparatively large affairs; he had about him an air of the great world; most important of all, he was professionally communicative and affable. The influence of such a man upon the customers of the place, all of whom were bidden to drink and permitted to converse with him, was necessarily for the good."

334. *Der Einzige und sein Eigenthum:* Published in America as *The Ego and His Own*, this is the one great work of Max Stirner (1806–56), the nihilist individualist. *Der Einzige*, an attack on all systems of morality, was such a bombshell that it brought café philosophizing in Berlin to an absolute halt while all the young radicals penned replies. We see in this letter an echo of the

loon-keepers' wives as Christmas presents, greatly to the scandal of the trade. When his kidneys gave out he was canned, and passed his last years as a pensioner on his son-in-law, Heinrich Gottlob. His funeral was notable. The cortege reached the Zionsgemeinde[335] cemetery, on the Harford Road, in a blinding snowstorm, but no less than eight Reds insisted upon making speeches, and so the ceremony lasted four hours. In fear of pneumonia, the mourners then rushed post-haste to Adam Dieterich's *Gasthaus*, and some of them remained there, hugging the stove and drinking *Kognak*,[336] until the next afternoon. Adam once told me that he took in sixty-seven dollars from them, of which about sixty dollars, he said, was profit. A few weeks later his wife, Minna, appeared at the Arbeiter Liedertafel's *Kinderbal*[337] (with her young daughter Emma) in the most gorgeous black silk ever turned out by Mrs. Schnur, the estimable modiste.

But do you remember Tillie Zinkhand?

Mencken

Dear Mencken:

Did I know Tillie Zinkhand? Long, long before you ever dreamed of her. When the old man died—he had a retail shoe

---

ideas of James Gibbons Huneker, ideas that Mencken imbibed along with the Pilsner at Lüchow's restaurant. Stirner was a favorite of Huneker, and was alloted a chapter in his *Essays*.

335. Zionsgemeinde: Zion congregation.

336. *Kognak:* Cognac, brandy.

337. *Kinderbal:* Children's dance.

store in Hanover, Pa.—Mama Zinkhand reasoned it out that there was no chance for a girl like Tillie in a small town, so after the estate was settled they moved down to Baltimore, Mama taking that big house on East Baltimore Street for just a few nice, refined boarders. What with the lodge money and the Sick Benefit Fund, Old Gustav left something over three thousand dollars, which Mama invested in furniture, linens and silverware. Kaan's,[338] from whom she bought the stuff, had a place on Broadway in those days, and it was through one of the Buyers that Tillie subsequently met Ludwig Emmerich. Ludwig, as you probably know, was still in mourning for his first wife when he met Tillie, and it evoked no little comment when Sunday after Sunday he was seen with her at Dr. Schneider's church. It was about this time that he went to live with the Zinkhands and Mama used to say to the other boarders that she looked upon Ludwig "just as if he was one of the family." So did Tillie, but for other reasons.

Some of the others who lived at Zinkhand's at various times were Hugo Wolff and his wife who was Minna Schlegel, Chris and Willy Heimgaertner, who were bachelors and knew the Zinkhands from Hanover where years before they had sold them goods, Hermann Dekker and his family, and Fred Spaeth. Fred was madly in love with Tillie and appeared to be making some headway the summer that Ludwig went back to Bautzen[339] to see his mother. But upon Ludwig's return she

338. Kaan's reminds us of Kann's, a well-known Baltimore department store of the last century. The story, as with all of these tales, is fictitious, but Goodman gives his store a name reminiscent of the era.

339. Bautzen: Manufacturing center near Dresden.

suddenly grew very cool, and poor Fritz [Fred Spaeth] moved away. Mama Zinkhand raised hell with her for trifling with him as she did. The room remained empty all of that winter and a part of the next spring, a fact which Mama always interpreted as a Divine stricture. In fact, it remained empty until it was taken by Louis Ebberle, and when he left suddenly, owing for three weeks, Mama was certain that she felt God's inscrutable hand. Ill-luck continued to pursue them until at last Mama ended the matter by moving into the room herself.

Goodman

Dear Goodman:

Not Minna Schlegel, *Kerl*,[340] but *Emma*. Minna was the fat aunt, already dead in 1883. Emma I knew very well. Her father owned the great orchestrion[341] in Frederick Street—a marvel of the eighties. All visitors went to see it, and stayed to drink little George Bauernschmidt's *Helles*[342] and to wolf the *Heringsalat* at the end of the long bar. Emma and I were in the same classes at Knapp's. She had a temper—and long pigtails. Many a time have I pulled 'em on drowsy afternoons, and made her squeal, and got my buttocks fanned by Herr Paul, the professor of penmanship, single entry bookkeeping, art, geography, spelling, German poetry, long division, the Franco-Prussian war, and calisthenics.

340. *Kerl:* Fellow, chap.
341. Orchestrion: Large music box or barrel organ, capable of imitating various instruments.
342. *Helles:* Pale ale.

Mama Zinkhand died in 1899, and the *pension* was taken over by a Viennese lady, Frau Darsch. Along about 1903 she was taken in adultery with Hermann Decker (not Dekker), and Hermann's wife, Kunigunde, floored her with a flat-iron. The thing got into the papers and made a great scandal. I have even been told that Pastor Batz preached upon it at his church in Highlandtown, taking his text from the passage denouncing the Hoor of Babylon. Soon afterward Frau Darsch disappeared and the old house was converted into a Talmud Torah school by the Congregation Bar Mitzveh, or some such name. All I remember is the name of the rabbi, Dr. Silberstern.

But do you remember Dr. Siegfried Kellerman, the famous Gay Street obstetrician? Or Olga Bernau, who married Fritz Bartels, the accordion player, and went with him under the name of the Two Harmonic Hendersons? Or Julius Tiemeyer, who committed suicide by jumping into the mash-vat at the Lion brewery? Or Jake Middendorf, the dog trainer?

Mencken

Dear Mencken:

I remember Dr. Kellerman by name only. Dr. Bernard Fischer served our family in that capacity. Fischer was a stern homeopath. Above his desk hung a large portrait of Hahnemann.[343]

343. Samuel Hahnemann (1755–1843) founded homeopathy, the treatment of disease with drugs that, in a healthy person, would produce the symptoms of the disease. Some of Hahnemann's more ridiculous ideas, though later discarded by his disciples, left a lingering doubt about the soundness of his meth-

He never married, but gossip always mumbled something about him and Mrs. Steglich the wet-nurse whom he would recommend in his important cases.

When Mrs. Steglich died, a Mrs. Pfaumuller took her place, and a very capable woman she was. Lily Obst, after a dozen premature operations by Dr. Fischer, was finally deprived of his services because of his warm friendship for her husband. Then it was that Lily began cuddling up to Mrs. Pfaumuller and thereafter the attentions of the Doctor were no longer required. With this assurance, life became worthwhile to Lily and young Arno Leonhardt. Arno's father, old Ernst Leonhardt, was in on the secret, and often, with a sly wink and an encouraging slap, would say to Arno that he was his father all over again. The Leonhardts were Berliners![344]

Olga Bernau who married Fritz Bartels was Chris Stegmaier's daughter. When Chris had been dead but a year, his widow married Bernau, and Olga, still very young, assumed her step-father's name. And you say that the female Harmonic Henderson is none other than little Olga. It seems incredible. I must tell Nathan.

But do you remember Henry Lierz who, for many years with Mrs. Lierz, led the Grand March at the *Junger Maennerchor's*[345] Annual Charity Ball? Lierz was a cigar manufacturer

---

ods. This mixture of quackery and compassionate healing appealed to Goodman's imagination.

344. Berliners are, of course, assumed to be sophisticates.

345. *Junger Maennerchor:* Young men's chorus.

and, if memory doesn't trick me, called his five cent leader the "Baron Steuben."[346] Am I right?

Goodman

[Dec. 25, 1918]

Dear Goodman:

Mrs. Steglich the *wet* nurse? Good God! She was no more a wet-nurse than that moving-picture Goldfish;[347] she had been dry since her Hermann was weaned, in 1877. She was a *Geburtshülferin*,[348] and a very good one. I am ashamed of you. Old Dr. Buddenbohn used to say that Mrs. Steglich was better than the largest pair of forceps then known. She had an almost uncanny skill at coaxing the reluctant young into this sorrowful vale. She got out Tillie Linsenmeyer's twins in two hours and eight minutes, and had Tillie on her feet again and ironing Fritz's shirts within eleven days.

---

346. The Baron Steuben cigar celebrates Friedrich Wilhelm August, Baron von Steuben (1730–94), the Prussian general who helped Washington at Valley Forge. American cigars were a continuing Mencken interest; the *Mercury* ran a history in the May 1924 issue.

347. "moving-picture Goldfish": Samuel Goldfish changed his name this year (1918) to Goldwyn, and was later the head of Samuel Goldwyn Productions in Hollywood. Mencken and Goodman discussed the phenomenon of Jews changing their names to something more acceptable in America. Samuel Goldfish was one of these stories. Many studios still had their primary offices in New York in 1918, and for this reason the studios interested Mencken and Goodman even if their product was not yet intellectually respectable. "The squads of lovely movie gals, to my bucolic eye, looked like princesses or even like angels," wrote Mencken.

348. *Geburtshülferin:* Midwife.

Of her contrary activities—that is, the interest of ladies suffering from inadvertence[349] and extra-legal pregnancies—I know little, but I daresay she let no meritorious appeal go unanswered. She had a big heart; also, an astounding development of the mammalia. Such a bust, indeed, was quite marvelous.

Henry Lierz I knew very well. The Baron Steuben, however, was a ten-center—pure Havana. His five-cent leader was the Helmuth von Moltke[350]—a very bad smoke. He always donated one hundred at Christmas to the German Orphan Asylum. They were smoked, of course, not by the orphans, but by the directors (i. e., Karl Schweinfurth, *Vorsitzer;*[351] Gottlieb Gegner, Adolph Knatz, Hugo Thiernauer, Wilhelm Schlens and Wilhelm Blankenagel). They always gave half a dozen to Gustave, the janitor. What his other name was, no one ever knew. He was always plain Gustave. He was wounded at Wörth and belonged to the *Kriegerbund.*[352]

Today is Christmas. It was on Christmas, 1894, that the

---

349. "inadvertence": Unplanned pregnancy. Midwives were sometimes asked to help women with abortions and sometimes they undertook these "contrary activities."

350. Helmuth von Moltke (1800–1891), a Prussian field marshal. His triumphs against Austria and France (1866–70) were decisive steps toward German unification. Mencken delights in the incongruity: the sainted name of von Moltke applied to a bad five-cent cigar. For generations the family's patriotic service continued, and the last of the line, Helmuth James von Moltke, was executed in 1945 for opposition to Hitler.

351. *Vorsitzer:* Chairman.

352. Wörth: The Battle of Wörth (1870) was a bloody Prussian victory in the Franco-German war. *Kriegerbund:* Veterans club.

beautiful Anna Marie Hofmeister was married to Kuno Bingel, that *Schuft!*[353] I'll never forget her.

Mencken

Dear Mencken:

Somewhere I have read that you wear low button shoes;[354] consequently I am not amazed that you should make the statement that Anna Hofmeister was beautiful. That you may know my taste in such matters, I ask you to close your eyes and dream back upon the faces of such lovely creatures as Sadie Stroebel, Frieda Vollrath, Minna Altmaier, Clara Volz, Emma Gindele and that Klagholz girl whose front name now escapes me. There were real beauties for you! Not alone was Anna not beautiful, but she was as dumb as *gritz.*[355] On the very morning of her wedding her mama threatened to give her a *"potch"* as big as her hand because of her intention to wear the same *unterhosen* that she had been wearing all that week.[356] Then she went off in a corner to *"shmull"*[357] and blurted out that she was only marrying Kuno Bingel because her papa wanted her to. Fortunately only the family heard the remark.

353. *Schuft:* Scoundrel. The name Bingel is cognate with Bengel, meaning "rascal," which certainly fits Kuno.

354. Button shoes lingered in Mencken's wardrobe into the 1920s. He complained that he could not tie laces.

355. *Gritz:* Grits, mush.

356. *"potch":* A slap, the mark made by a slap. *Unterhosen:* Underpants, knickers.

357. *"shmull":* Sulk.

I hold no brief for Kuno Bingel—God knows after what he did to your uncle Anton Biebl he could get no sympathy from me—but in strict justice could he be seriously blamed for beating hell out of Anna? Why her own father even refused to take her part. *Schuft* he was, I grant you, but a *Schuft* has his rights.

That escapade of Kuno's with Hermann Ebbecke's wife is another instance where he was painted blacker that the facts warranted. While the testimony showed that he had demanded thirty dollars of her under penalty of exposing his relations with her to her husband, it was also clearly set forth that they had been intimate for over a year and a half before that. Indeed, the evidence of the case showed that she had been making a sucker of him, and that not until he was flat did he ever demand a cent of her. Scruple be damned! Picture yourself in the fellow's place.

No, there was something about Kuno that regrettably reveals that under other conditions he might have been a better man. Take the Commercial Hotel fire in Hagerstown for example. What he did that night in the face of death I can never forget. While I was not there, I had it from Chief Gebbartsbauer's own lips that Kuno personally accounted for three lives.

What has become of all the old members of the *Schützen Verein*[358] that defeated the Philadelphia gunners at Handel & Haydn Park in the summer of 1897? On the team, as far as I can recall, were Joe Straubmuller, Hans Weniger, Charlie Him-

---

358. *Schützen Verein:* Shooting club. We are reminded that Baltimore's Schützen-gesellschaft was a popular social club, with a large park featuring bowling, dancing, and festive bibbing and eating.

merlein, Gus Schwoerer, Chris Widmaier, Otto Troescher, Henry Helbling, Adam Ostertag and Carl Vollrath, father of the glorious Frieda. And did Mrs. Muellershoen ever get damages from the club when one of the waiters accidentally spilled some beer on her, ruining her black satin dress? Those were the days—*and the nights!* Do you remember the Saturday night when everyone started for home and Fred Doeppel's wife and Louis Woehr were missing from the party? Then began a search of the woods for a quarter of a mile around. Poor Fred was white from fear. Charlie Himmerlein made a very nasty remark that almost caused a free fight then and there. About half past twelve, the missing couple came trooping back, Clara Doeppel having a most suspicious attack of giggles. Fred put his arms around her neck and kissed her. The bunch wanted to know where they had been. Louis replied that they had been hunting for four leaf clovers by moonlight!!!

Goodman

Dear Goodman:

I had heard of your Liberty Loan work. Karl Blaetzner showed me the ads you drew up for the *Lutherische Wochenfreund.*[359] He told me, however, that he had no cut of Gen. von Pershing, and so used an old one of Gen. von Kluck.[360] I suggested a change,

359. *Lutherische Wochenfreund:* Newspaper, the *Lutheran Weekly Friend.*
360. Gen. John Pershing (1860–1948) was, of course, no German. He commanded the American Expeditionary Force, 1917–19. Gen. Alexander von Kluck (1846–1934) commanded the German invasion of France, 1914. The irony is intended.

and hope you will approve—that is, to print *Freiheits Lehne*[361] in 72-point Gothic.

It will interest you to know that Wilhelm Darsch, late of the *Badener Chemikalische-Fabrik*,[362] has invented a new synthetic chewing-gum containing neither sugar nor gum. It can be made for two marks[363] a kilo in quantities. Old Lorenz Schaffner, president of the Chemnitzer Bauverein,[364] is organizing a company to manufacture it, and has rented the Ilgenfritz Pilsner Brewery, now dismantled. His son-in-law, Lawyer Bernhard Gast, will be chief counsel to the company, at a retainer of $400 a year. Bertha will now get that new Stieff upright piano.

Mencken

Dear Mencken:

Recently there came to light an old dance card of mine dated Thursday evening, February 18, 1892, the occasion being the Fourteenth Annual Ball of the Junger Maennerchor[365] at Harmonie Hall. The music was furnished by Prof. Haertel's Or-

---

361. *Freiheits Lehne:* Liberty Loan, the sale of bonds to finance the American war effort. This would have received a lukewarm reception in the German community. Mencken knew that Goodman was most decidedly not supporting the patriotic fervor.

362. *Badener Chemikalische-Fabrik:* Baden Chemical Factory.

363. Two marks: Fifty cents.

364. *Chemnitzer Bauverein:* Chemnitz Building Society.

365. *Junger Maennerchor:* Young men's chorus.

chestra (greatly augmented); the dances, selections and names of my partners follow:

I. (Overture) Raymond
II. Waltz: "Morning, Noon and Night in Vienna" (with) Julia Lustgarte
III. Two-steps: "High School Cadets" (with) Edelgard Fuerth
IV. Schottische: "Bonn Studentenlied" (with) Hedwig Woeffel
V. Waltz: "Arias from Waldteufel" (with) Gretchen Bauschmeyer

Intermission

VI. Waltz: "Artist's Life" (with) Edelgard Fuerth
VII. Lancers: "Black Eagle" (with) Edelgard Fuerth
VIII. Two-step: "Poor Jonathan" (with) Anna Kraus
IX. Waltz: "A Bicycle Built for Two" (with) Edelgard Fuerth
X. Finale: "Heigh Lee—Heigh Lo" (with) Edelgard Fuerth

I lost my heart that night as my program attests. In fact it was always a mystery to me that she received my attentions as she did, for she was secretly engaged at the time to young Dr. Georg Reisholz. Later their engagement was broken off and she married Christian Volkmar. This Volkmar, by the way, was a brother of the famous Volkmar who invented the Saloon Lunch Slot Machine. I have not seen Edelgard since her wedding. I think of her often and wonder if she is still the will-o'-

the-wisp creature I once loved. . . . It is true that she has seven children!

Goodman

Dear Mencken:

And it now turns out that Carl Boecherer never became a citizen. Those papers that he asked you to witness some years ago were not Naturalization Blanks but Claim Forms of the Aetna Accident Company of Hartford. He was working for J. Schroeder & Sons at the time and one of Schroeder's nephews, Mark Littmer, wrote him up for a $15,000 accident policy. Two days after the policy was delivered Carl was mysteriously hurt in a lathe press. He claimed twenty-six weeks total disability and it was allowed. That was the summer that he took his family to Mauch Chunk[366] and stopped at the Highland House in a great style. . . . So you always believed that they were Naturalization Papers. . . . Well, well!

The local Red Cross[367] teams captained by Christian Zupp and Sigmund Milch respectively are in the lead at this writing. Zupp is a genius in matters of organization. With the aid of his capable young field manager, Gottlieb Gelb, he has members of the Moltke Lodge stationed at every remaining saloon on

366. Mauch Chunk is a town in eastern Pennsylvania. In 1954 it was renamed Jim Thorpe, as a memorial to the great American Indian athlete (1888–1953) who was an Olympic standout in 1912.

367. The Red Cross, raising money for American soldiers, was the most popular patriotic charity among German-Americans because the money went solely for humanitarian causes.

Second and Third Avenue north of Fifty-ninth Street importuning customers to take one drink less and make one contribution more. The idea was really not his, Past Master Wilhelm Bechtold having first suggested the plan, but who other than Zupp could have put it into practical execution?

Goodman

May 14 [1919]

Dear Goodman:

The Franz Abt *Bauverein*[368] somehow has an evil name. It surely must be well known to you that during the regime of Hermann's father, old Otto Moll, the association was not above lending money upon public stews.[369]

I was once told by Miss Irene LeMoine herself that Otto had advanced her $3,000 upon her public pay station in Watson Street. True enough, the house was worth $6,000, and Irene did a business of $700 a week, but all the same the principle was bad. Much of the money of the *Verein* came from church people—members of Pastor Oehlenshläger's Martinikirche.[370] The whole thing came out when the Pastor's boy, Rudolph, was robbed in the house and complained to the police. The *Deutsche Correspondent* featured the scandal for weeks.

The Metzger Liedertafel has resumed rehearsals under

---

368. *Bauverein:* Building loan society.
369. "public stews": Brothels.
370. *Verein:* Building society. Martinikirche: St. Martin's Lutheran Church.

Prof. Schneidereith. The first large work to be given will be Knortz's *"Ein deutsches Heldenlied."*[371]

Mencken

July 2 [1919]

Dear Goodman:

I have a complete file of your letters. There is a good book in the "Do You Remember?" series.[372] Let us do it some time or other. I offer you, for your interest, the damage I have suffered by your sale of my books to Knopf.[373]

All I ask is that you not depict me as irreligious. Since I have become interested in Pastor Schneider's daughter Gusta I have had to put the soft pedal on atheism.

Knopf has been awarded the *Ordre Pour le Mérite*,[374] with palms, by the Oheb Shalom Congregation for horning you.[375] A case of Rhine wine goes with the award.

---

371. *"Ein deutsches Heldenlied"*: A German heroic song. Karl Knortz (1841–1918) was a prolific poet.

372. "a good book . . . ": Mencken suggests creating a book from these letters.

373. Alfred A. Knopf had taken over the publication of Mencken's books. Far from being damaged, Mencken was very happy with the arrangement, which lasted until his death in 1956.

374. *Ordre pour le Mérite:* A Prussian military decoration for individual gallantry in action. The decoration, in the shape of a Maltese cross, is worn on a black ribbon around the neck. There is a separate version for distinction in science and art.

375. "horning you": Getting the better of you. The implication is that Knopf got the better of Goodman in buying the unsold stock of Mencken's two titles, *Damn! A Book of Calumny* and *In Defense of Women*, not to mention getting Mencken himself for his list of authors.

Mrs. Berta Seibold, who has sold pot herbs in Hollins Market[376] for thirty-four years, has been summonsed for profiteering. The ladies' committee of Martini Evangelische Gemeinde[377] charge her with asking eighteen cents for a bunch of *Schnittlauche*.[378]

Mencken

July 8 [1919]

Dear Goodman:

Knopf is examining every book separately and personally.[379] When he bought out the Torah Publishing Company and took over the Sex Hygiene books of Dr. Maurice Hutzler, they worked off half a bale of toilet paper on him.

I met Sabina on July 17, 1907, and she was already in the hands of Dr. Eichenlaub by August 15.[380] It was an alfresco affair and hence careless. Please don't mention it in your article. She has six children by her husband, Pfannenbecker, and one by a druggist, by name Dr. Emil Hahn. All are well. Schnitkin, the shyster lawyer, was disbarred in 1914, and is now running the Philanthropic Low-Interest Chattel Mortgage Company in Exeter Street.

376. Hollins Market is a farmer's market down the street from Mencken's house.

377. Martini Evangelische Gemeinde: St. Martin's Lutheran Congregation.

378. *Schnittlauche:* Chives.

379. Mencken's joke. Knopf had bought the unbound sheets of Mencken's books from Goodman. Mencken jokes here that Knopf is examining all of them carefully to be sure they are not blank paper or worse.

380. "in the hands of Dr. Eichenlaub": The consequence of a careless fling was an unplanned pregnancy.

Franz Lobenschein has been released from Fort Oglethorpe,[381] and will resume his position as salesman for the
Schmidt Bros. Novelty Co., manufacturers of patriotic badges.

Mencken

July 16 [1919]

Dear Goodman,

If the Miss Pomerantz you mention is Miss Bertha, then old
Freundlich was played for a sucker. She is a veritable slave of
her passions. When she was bookkeeper for Max Friedenthal,
the small-time booking agent, it was a common saying that no
vaudeville actor got bookings in that office without standing
her a six-dollar dinner at the Astor and ministering to her illicit appetites afterward. Melvin Leventhal is a hypocrite if he
says he was unaware of this. He was office boy for Max at the
time, and the common gossip is that Bertha betrayed him and
then kept him. Such details are noisome, but the truth is the
truth—*Wahrheit ist Wahrheit!*

Karl Knortz, for twenty-seven years head bookkeeper at the
Pabst Baltimore branch, has retired to his farm at Bismark's
Switch, Md. He is worth $18,000. He will appreciate a picture
postcard now and then.

Yours, *Mencken*

---

381. Fort Oglethorpe in Georgia is referred to as a place where prisoners
are sent for disobeying the stringent patriotic laws of World War I. The anti-
German hysteria of that time inspires this letter. The irony in the remainder
of the sentence is deliberate.

July 21st [1919]

Dear Goodman:

It now turns out that Cox is a grandson of old Melchior Koch, for thirty years *Vorsitzer* of the Lebanon, Pa. *Liedertafel.*[382] It was at the funeral of the old gentleman that the Bach Choir was poisoned by the ptomained *Heringsalat.*[383]

Mencken

July 22nd [1919]

Dear Goodman:

In general, my advice is that it is cheaper to pay a little black-mail now and then than to fight it in the courts. After all, a man must expect to be mulcted for his carnalities. I set aside $100 a month and call it fair. The perils of making a row were well exemplified in the case of my uncle Ferdinand. After pay-ing the Widow Grunemann eight dollars a week for three years, he went into the courts of equity and demanded relief. He got it—but his lawyers got his house in West Lexington Street. Moreover, the news that he *had* paid hush-money to die Grunemannin stirred up half a dozen other wenches, and they demanded back salaries, so to speak. I know that at least one of them, Teenie Holzhauer, settled for $400. Ferdinand never got over it. With my own ears I heard him say on his deathbed that he wished some catastrophe of God had emasculated him in early life.

---

382. *Vorsitzer:* Chairman. *Liedertafel:* Choral society.

383. *Heringsalat:* Herring salad contains potatoes, onions, cream, and so on, which would spoil if left in a warm place.

If you doubt what I told you about my musical talents, go ask Prof. Siegmund Moll, conductor of the Westfälische Liedertafel.

Mencken

August 7th [1919]

Dear Goodman:

The decay of language in this great barbaric republic continues to excite my shuddering amazement. Amer ritter, indeed! *Was meinen Sie? Arme Ritter?*[384] I have et many a plate of it, with powdered sugar. A side dish of stewed *Erdbeeren* helps to make it tasty.

The recent election of Mayor Broening has drafted many of your friends into the public service.[385] Karl Horstmüller is now a school commissioner and Emil Krüger sits on the water board. The venerable Kuno Dorfendinger, who lost his bookkeeper's stool at the Anheuser-Busch Baltimore Branch when Methodism triumphed,[386] is now an auditor in the Building

---

384. *Arme Ritter,* or "Poor Knight," means dessert fritters. *"Was meinen Sie?"* ("What do you mean?") asks Mencken, in reply to Goodman's apparent typo. *Erdbeeren* are strawberries.

385. William Broening (1870–1953), elected mayor in 1918, was an oddity among Baltimore mayors—a Republican. Since Goodman and Mencken were Democrats, this is clearly a joke. Mencken has filled his list with marvelous German ethnic names, but Goodman's friends would certainly not be enlisted in a Republican administration. By coincidence, Baltimore was later to have a mayor named Philip Goodman (1959–63 term).

386. "Methodism triumphed": The Methodist Church led the movement for prohibition of alcoholic beverages.

Inspector's office. Old Adolf Aal's boy Raymond is in the Health Department as a privy inspector. And so it goes. I hear that Otto Schultze, who painted the famous Alpine scenes on the walls of Schneider's Family Café aspires to the Municipal Art Commission.

Mencken

August 29 [1919]

Dear Goodman:

It is amazing to observe the makings of a popular legend. Around the single fact that my venerable grandfather once broke his leg, the tongue of scandal has wrapped the Tiefenthaler funeral canard. The truth is that the accident occurred in 1862 and was caused by a sliver of *Blutwurst*[387] on the floor of the famous old-time family place of Ludwig Wiesbader. There was no hint of excessive bibbing at the time. The old man, then but thirty-seven years old, had dropped into the *Ausschank* to get his *Morgenschoppen*.[388] After exchanging

---

387. *Blutwurst:* Blood sausage. Blutwurst is so often implicated in falls that each instance must be examined for its mixture of truth and fiction. It is more fun in the retelling to blame the fictional blutwurst than a more mundane cause. For instance, Sara Mayfield, in *The Constant Circle* (New York: Delacorte Press, 1968), 189, reports that Goodman himself slipped on a piece of blutwurst and sprained his ankle during a visit to Sinclair Lewis and Dorothy Thompson's home, Twin Farms, in 1931. One can blame the story on Mencken, who was present at the time, and who probably embellished the tale in a letter, knowing that Goodman would enjoy being thus ennobled. The real story, reported in Mencken's *Diary* (28) is simply that Goodman "slipped on the house-step."

388. *Ausschank:* Pub. *Morgenschoppen:* Morning glass of beer. A *schoppen* is about one-half liter.

the time of day with Mamma Wiesbader, who always tended the bar from 8:00 A.M. to 11:00, he turned to go out, hoofed the *Blutwurst* and came down with a thud. Dr. Buddenbohm, the family physician, kept him on two canes until after the surrender at Appomattox. Hence his well-known failure to take any personal part in the battle for liberty—a piece of ill-fortune that was destined, half a century later,[389] to pursue all of his descendants.

Yours, *Mencken*

Dear Mencken:

Braunschweig Bros. of Hazleton[390] are adding a Crockery Department to their store and want to know the present whereabouts of that Schuldenfrei fellow who started a similar department for Kaan's many years ago. Can you oblige? For my part, I would not move a leg to do Sig Braunschweig a favor, for it was he who started that ugly gossip the summer that the

389. "Half a century later" means World War I. There could be lingering doubts of the family's patriotic zeal if grandfather Burkhardt Ludwig Mencken had been malingering to avoid the War Between the States. Mencken told his biographer, Isaac Goldberg, that his grandfather had, in fact, missed action on account of lameness due to a broken leg. We can dismiss the rest of the tale, however. For one thing, Mencken's grandfather did not become 37 until two months after Lee's surrender at Appomattox. And we should never take a blutwurst-myth at face value. If grandfather Mencken's patriotism were questioned it would actually arise from his preference for the South, a preference shared by many of his Baltimore neighbors. Cf. Goldberg, *The Man Mencken*, 53.

390. Hazleton is a manufacturing center 20 miles south of Wilkes-Barre, Pa.

Harmonie opened their fishing club at Essington.[391] In the first place, when Alonzo Knochenhauer, who was Chairman of the Amusement Committee, moved to buy the little shack he expressly stated that members' wives would necessarily be barred because of the fact that there were but four bedrooms in the place. You will remember that Braunschweig was furious at this piece of legislation and threatened to resign from the club. Instead, he gave wide circulation to a tale that women were not being barred—that is, a certain class of women, and went so far as to describe the carnality that was supposed to have gone on there. Naturally, the news reached the ears of Frau Knochenbauer with the result that Alonzo was forbidden to go down for his weekends. The same thing happened to Gus Reisenhofer and Emil Pfund. My God, argued the women folks, were they not all men of families? Why, such tales getting out would ruin them. In short, the Essington place went begging and the Harmonie was stuck for the rent for that entire Summer. That's your Braunschweig for you! If you want to do him a favor, go ahead.

Goodman

Sept. 3rd [1919]

Dear Goodman:

One may reasonably object to your inquiries, I fancy, on the ground of good taste, but it would surely be absurd to question the general accuracy of your reports. The Winterfelter

391. Essington is a town in southeast Pennsylvania on the Delaware River.

(not Winterfeldt) episode gave great grief to the judicious. The venerable man, though suffering at the time from a compound stricture with prostatic enlargement and thus quite incapable of crim. con.,[392] was nevertheless so flattered by the plaintiff's vivid description of the manner in which he had betrayed her on her parlor sofa that he insisted upon admitting the charge. His attorney, Lawyer Leopold Bierbauer, protested in vain. The damages were set at $1,800 plus costs, amounting in all to $2,762.50. I have the itemized statement of Advocate Bierbauer, with the attached quittance.[393]

But Schneider, himself surely no ascetic, refused the last rites for a quite different reason. His grounds were purely theological. He pointed out that the canon of the Prussian State Church absolutely forbade burying a professed atheist in consecrated ground. The most he would do was to say a prayer at the house and accept an invitation to the funeral dinner. He was then seventy-eight years of age, and one bottle of Rülander[394] put him to sleep. The actual services were conducted by Pastor Gottfried Borst, of the Martini Congregation. It was generally believed that this Borst was a natural son of Pastor Schneider. At all events, he did all of the old man's dirty work. His putative father, Georg Friedrich Borst, was a ne'er-do-well, and the first member of the Arbeiter Liedertafel ever to

392. "crim. con.": "Criminal conversation," legal term for illicit sex. For comic effect, Mencken has exaggerated the effect of prostatic enlargement: it might interfere with urination, but would not preclude sexual intercourse.

393. Quittance: Legal document showing that the judgment was paid.

394. Rülander: Wine of Germany, little known for a generation because it comes from what was East Germany.

read *Das Kapital.*[395] By profession he was a polisher of piano legs, but he seldom worked. Old Man Wilhelm Knabe used to say that he was the damnedest *Schuft* ever employed in the Knabe piano factory.

Yours, *Mencken*

Sept. 9 [1919]

Dear Goodman:

One embraces the lesser scandal to silence the greater. A man of sixty-five loses nothing by being accused of crim. con.; nine people of ten envy him. But I naturally say nothing, save in the utmost privacy, and to trusted friends, about the famous Mencken-Garfinkel suit. It is true enough that Garfinkel was a fraud and that his Syrian Sultan brand of Egyptian cigarettes was actually made of Pennsylvania ground-leaves, but nevertheless I feel that Grandpa went too far when he sold the fellow that carload of Lancaster County filler.[396] It had been stored in the cellar of the old Burgmein malt warehouse in Sharp Street.[397] There was an old privy well in the cellar and at the time of the 1889 flood it overflowed and drenched the whole stock with excreta.

395. Arbeiter Liedertafel: Workers choral society. *Das Kapital:* Karl Marx's seminal book about capital and communism. Everything paints old man Borst as a scoundrel, and the name literally means "bristle brush," a traditional nickname for a snappish person.

396. Ground-leaves: The lowest tobacco leaves are poor quality and do not make a good cigarette. Lancaster County, in southeast Pennsylvania, was not only a center of German settlement, but an important tobacco-growing region.

397. Sharp Street in Baltimore, near the harbor.

The old man sold the whole stock to Garfinkel at eight cents, sight unseen, falsely misrepresenting himself to be caught in a leaf panic. When Garfinkel put the stuff into cigarettes and his customers began to smoke them, there was hell to pay. The old gentleman's lawyer, Attorney Baumgartner, made the jury laugh by imitating Garfinkel's dialect, and so the verdict was for but three cents. Nevertheless, I have always felt that Garfinkel had the better of it: eventually, he got his money back. That is, he applied for the benefit of the bankruptcy laws and got out at 4 cents on the dollar. It was a few months later that his wife bought the handsome house on Eutaw Place, now a center of Ashkenazim revelry.[398] His granddaughter, Mae Garfield,[399] has been to Vassar and is the moving spirit in one of the local "art" theatres. She is reported to be engaged to Irving Hutzler. Old Garfinkel died worth $200,000 and left money to finish the dome on the Oheb Shalom synagogue. His only male descendant, Sidney Garfield, is a famous atheist.

Yours, *Mencken*

398. Eutaw Place, north of the city center, Baltimore. Ashkenazim: The Jews from northern Europe.

399. The change of name to Garfield emphasizes the family's assimilation into the American mainstream. At this time Mencken, finishing *The American Language*, was studying the Americanization of surnames. "For a hundred years past all the heaviest and most degrading labor of the United States has been done by successive armies of foreigners, and so a concept of inferiority has come to be attached to mere foreignness" (*The American Language*, 1st ed. [1919], 278).

Dear Goodman:

Paul Zerbst deserves all his luck. For sixteen years he slaved in his drug-store, never making more than $1,800 a year. He owes the formula of the Ponce de Leon[400] tablets to old Dr. Scharnagel. The doctor, on his deathbed, gave it to him, with a written quitclaim.[401] It is actually a meritorious article. You will recall Wilhelm Horst and his wife, *geb.* Tiemeyer, and their pathetic longing for offspring. Well, Wilhelm went on the pills for three days, and two weeks later Tillie was overdue. Young Dr. Raymond Scharnagel, who studied in Vienna, says that he is convinced, by the foetal sounds, that it will be a boy. Wilhelm is in a magnificent frame of mind.

I got the [Jewish] New Year card. It was very tasty.

Mencken

Oct. 14, 1919

Dear Goodman:

Your naturally keen mind, I take it, grasped the nature of my engagement. It was, of course, with Fraulein X. A charming gal. If you had risked the twenty-seven cents for a telegram I might have stalled her off. As it was, a last moment excuse would have shocked her, and perhaps affected her health. She is a girl of strong emotions.

I hear that the Rodof Sholom Congregation has offered

---

400. Juan Ponce de Leon (1460?–1521), while searching for the Fountain of Youth, found Florida. On his second trip he was killed by the natives.

401. Quitclaim: A conveyance of ownership.

$8,000 cash, with $17,500 remaining on the mortgage, for the edifice of the Beulah Baptist Church in Stiles Street. All the Baptists have moved away from the neighborhood and the church has been dark since 1916. It was the scene, as you may recall, of a great revival in 1884. During this revival no less than 260 *Kandidaten*[402] were ducked in the tank, and the evangelist, Rev. Smith, was under water so much that he came down with pleurisy.

I see Dr. Groskopf very often. He is a fine old man, and when he walks along East Baltimore Street in his plug hat and long alpaca coat he always reminds me of Abraham. He still does his marketing in Belair Market, and the butchers and hucksters say that it is impossible to fool him.

Mencken

Dear Goodman:

I have been wanting to tell you about your Uncle Heinrich for some time, but I seem not to be able to grab off a spare moment. However, you granted that he chewed slippery elm.[403] But do you remember the gold folding tooth-pick and ear-digger he carried in his vest pocket? And have you forgotten the pearl penknife with the little peep-hole through which one beheld, greatly magnified and in colors, the Alster Pavilion[404] in

402. *Kandidaten:* Candidates for church membership.
403. Slippery elm: The bark of this elm variety is chewed to soothe the throat.
404. The Alster Pavilion is a decorative building, housing a café, on the inner harbor.

Hamburg? That he wore mittens in winter sewed to a long piece of black tape which passed through both sleeves; that his favorite stein was the one with the transparent illustration in the bottom which, when held to the light, revealed Herr Tell[405] in front of an inn at Basel; that he carried his watch in an ebony outer case—all these, of course, are well known to you.

Mencken

Dear Mencken:

Ludwig Danziger and his nephew Paul Shulhoff are in town. They were at the Bismark the other night with the Pretzfelders, formerly of your city. Ludwig lost his wife last December. You never wrote a word about it. As they were childless, Paul is now his only consolation. Minnie Pretzfelder whispered to me—but this is in confidence—that she was trying to make a *shuttich*[406] between Ludwig and one of the Hofmeister girls. And why not? Ludwig is still young, and a decent fellow as men go. By the way, Ernie Pretzfelder tells me that he sold your mother your first pair of heeled shoes in his father's store.

He asked Ludwig what you were doing and that *Narr*[407] answered that he thought you were an accountant or something because you do so much writing at home.

Waldemar Eisenlohr was brought back from the Presbyter-

---

405. Herr Tell: Swiss hero William Tell, another proof of Uncle Heinrich's lowbrow taste.
406. *Shuttich:* Match. Often written "shidach."
407. *Narr:* Fool, buffoon.

ian Hospital this week with a glass tube in his left kidney. What a pathetic sight he is as he languishes in the home of his brother-in-law, George Oberfelder. At forty-four his days are few, the victim of American beer.[408]

The other night at the Bismark, Frieda Hetzel came over to our table. She has eight children *unberufen!*[409] Her eldest, Max, is now in France with our forces. She's the same Frieda, and tells a smutty story as well as ever she did. Her husband, by the way, comes from your city. Doubtless you know him—Bernhard Ellenbogen. He's a nephew of Dr. Brautwein, the chiropodist, and was brought up in the Doctor's household. He is with the Gelzer & Raab Malting Company and handles Pennsylvania, Ohio, and West Virginia. I hear they are very happy.

Goodman

Dear Mencken:

Charlotta Glaenzer, with whom you were confirmed, now the wife of Augie Gansemeyer, is visiting her aunt, Mrs. Kleinhanz of this city. I met the whole family the other night at the Bismark on 86th Street. Lotta's sister, Mrs. Hufnagel, is in a

---

408. American beer: German and Czech beers were cut off by the war, and beer drinkers suffered the consequences. Mencken later suggested that a lack of Pilsner, "the old elixir," may have hastened the death of James Huneker. Huneker had reported from London that "genuine Pilsner from Bohemia . . . has expelled the sugar from my blood!" But, Mencken sadly noted, "when he got back to Brooklyn there was only tea to drink, and so the sugar returned, and soon the news began to go about that the old boy was done for" (*Essays by James Gibbons Huneker*), x.

409. *Unberufen:* "May nothing happen." A charm.

precarious state at Johns Hopkins in your city, with carcinoma of the uterus. As you know, this trouble rarely presents itself except among spinsters. Let's see, does this not coincide with the fact that Fritz Hufnagel sustained a serious injury a month after he was married when he fell from his horse? From that time on he went into a decline. There were never any children. . . . The case is very plain to me. . . .

Leon Lubinsky wants to know if you would interest yourself in behalf of his thirteen year old boy, Tascha. He says that you heard him play the violin last winter and pronounced the opinion that he gave every promise of a great career. Moritz Rubenstein, himself a pupil of the famous Josephy,[410] says that the boy shows a more marked advancement at this age than Elman[411] did when he first appeared in public.

Leon thinks that you might be willing to write a few letters to the right people. He is in sore need of funds and is rather depending upon the boy's future concert engagements. He is no longer with Ginsberg Brothers, feeling that garment cutting is hardly compatible with the circle that Tascha is now moving in. Elkan Fishbein, his brother-in-law, refuses to advance another dollar. He is furious that Leon gave up his job.

Would you be willing to advance $500 if he gave you a con-

410. Josephy: Rafael Joseffy (1852–1915), the Hungarian concert pianist, made a teaching career in the United States. James Gibbons Huneker found the playing of this "thrice wonderful wizard" irresistible, and was for a time his student. Goodman may hark back to sessions where he heard Huneker describe the great pianist.

411. Elman: Apparently Mischa Elman (1891–1967), the Russian Jewish violinist, who became a U.S. citizen in 1923. See H. L. Mencken, *A Second Mencken Chrestomathy* (New York: Knopf, 1995), 171.

tract in writing calling for 25% of the boy's earnings for the next five years? He wants a fur-lined overcoat for the nearing winter, not, be assured, to gratify his own vanity, but for the greater managerial weight that it would lend. Tascha's interests are always foremost in his mind. If you could see your way clear to help him, it is my personal opinion that you would not alone have an excellent investment, but would be helping the cause of Art. I await your answer and hope that the proposition may receive your favorable consideration.

Goodman

Dear Mencken:

Everything seems to be going against the Lubinskys. Tascha's violin, the gift of his Uncle Slobodkin, was mysteriously stolen from their rooms late yesterday afternoon. It was our first impulse to notify the police, but Leon counseled against such hasty action. He argued that probably the thief might become repentant and return it. Such things have happened. He then opened a package containing a half dozen bottles of Slivovitz, which, he said, Margolies the Liquor Man on the corner had made him a present of in recognition of Tascha's genius.[412]

By the way, if you can arrange to have that $500 here by Saturday noon, Leon is willing to raise the percentage of Tascha's future earnings to 40%. Now, Bernie Berkovitz only

---

412. The appearance of the Slivovitz may be connected to the disappearance of the violin. Indeed, Uncle Slobodkin's gift of the violin may not have been appreciated, after all. This is one of Goodman's short sketches of human character.

got 40% when he loaned Leon $1000 six months ago, and I know that his contract with Morris Kaplan for a loan of $850 calls for only 30%. So you can see that you're getting the best of the bargain and, besides, your money is perfectly safe.

Goodman

Dear Mencken:

Old Anselm Hochblatt is dead. I had fears that the poor fellow would not get a decent burial—his children had become estranged because of his second marriage—but the Maimonides Talmud Torah Association has generously offered a funeral consisting of two carriages besides the hearse. Extra carriages may be had by mourners at the rate of nine dollars for the round-trip from the synagogue to the cemetery. Rabbi Asher Immerfeldt will officiate. Do not waste money on a floral tribute. I hear that everything will be in charge of *Shamus* Klonower whose son-in-law, Myer Rovnow, sells cut-price flowers to department stores. Klonower is Myer's chief source of supply. It is said that the both of them cleared over $300 on the Rosenblatt funeral. Luckily for them it was just at a time when immortelles were fetching big prices.

Dr. Boris Skodolev, late Professor of Post Biblical Literature at the University of Odessa, asks me if I think you would be willing to write a preface to his forthcoming History of Levantine Literature in the Third Century, Nicholas Murray Butler[413]

413. Nicholas Murray Butler (1862–1947), American educator who wrote about education and world affairs, was president of Columbia University from 1902 to 1945. Goodman may have known that Mencken was skeptical about

having refused. The Doctor, by the way, brings greetings to your family from old friends back in your native Irkutsk.[414]

Goodman

March 8 ⌈1920⌉

Dear Goodman:

I am astounded to hear that you are still alive. It is now just eighteen months since Lena Gerstbach went into mourning. With her own lips she told me the story of your heroic death at Château Thierry,[415] and of your honorable promise to marry her upon demobilization. No one blamed her a bit. If she yielded a bit too much, perhaps, to the moonlight and your artful caressing of her person, then it was a pure love that prompted her. The baby was born January 7, 1919. Pastor Hugendubel[416] made no bones about christening it. It bears the names of Philip and Erich, the first in memory of your gallant sacrifice and the last in honor of Gen. von Ludendorff.[417] Now you come back, ah God!

Butler, hence the allusion. Later "Nicholas Murray Butler—Portrait of a Reactionary" appeared in the *American Mercury* for March 1935.

414. Irkutsk, Siberia, was a place of banishment.

415. Château-Thierry (June-July 1918) was one of the first victories of the American troops in France. French commander Foche, aided by the American Expeditionary Force, turned the tide of the war in this battle.

416. Hugendubel: if taken apart into *Hügen* + *Dübel* the name means "think of the devil."

417. Erich von Ludendorff: German general of the world war, subject both of Mencken's admiration and an article he wrote for the *Atlantic Monthly* in June 1917.

Let Reisholz be damned: Uncle Theodor is the *Schuft* of the family. Surely you don't expect me to make good all his small swindlings. He died in August 1918, of *Leberkrankheit*.[418] He was buried by Scharnhorst Lodge, No. 74, A. F. & A. M.

If you have seen the Niteschy,[419] you beat me. Noff seldom sends me any of my own books. Can't I borrow your copy?

   Mencken

Dear Mencken:

And that brings me up to Old Man Kupferschmidt, whose death I learn of for the first time. With his demise who will care for his eldest sister, *Tante* Gretchen, who was many years his senior? Kupferschmidt had no children, but there were nieces and nephews from the Falk branch of the family. Will they provide for her? I doubt it. She burned her bridges in that split-up in 1894—or was it '95?—when Julius Falk threatened his brother-in-law, Kupferschmidt, if he did not go through with his promise made to the poor *Witwe*[420] Traubmann. It was then that *Tante* Gretchen came forward with the secret that Falk himself and the Traubmann woman had had an affair

---

418. *Leberkrankheit:* Liver disease, that is, cirrhosis, from heavy drinking.

419. "Niteschy . . . Noff": The misspelling is deliberate. Mencken is apparently referring to his translation of *The Antichrist*, which was published by Knopf in 1920. Mencken's fun with "Niteschy" follows an incident in 1917 when Mencken was accused of being a German spy and, more than that, a friend of "Nitsky, the German monster." Of course Mencken wouldn't have been a friend of Nietzsche, who died in 1900.

420. *Witwe:* Widow. *Tante:* Aunt.

twenty years before. Indeed, at the time, she said right to Julius's face that there was a suspicious resemblance between young Hermann Traubmann and himself. That was the night that Julius ordered her out of his house and they never spoke thereafter. So what can she expect from the Falk children? Once she told me that she used to love your grandmother *selig's Kartoffelklösse.*[421] . . .

Untermeyer and Held are at sea as to who should be included in their book of American poets,[422] or rather who should not be. So I have asked Mendel Rosenzweig, Wolf Louchheim and Benno Wohlegemuth to serve as an Advisory Committee.[423] I would also have asked Selig Hanauer, but he now is in the B'nai Brith Home and seldom leaves his room.

Goodman

May 22nd [1920]

Dear Goodman:

Old Frau Agathe Semmel has just died at the *Allgemeines-greisenheim,*[424] aet. eighty-nine. She was the *Kartoffelsalat*[425] champion of champions, and had made more than 10,000 tons

---

421. *Selig:* Blessed, of blessed memory. The honorific follows the name. *Kartoffelklösse:* Potato dumplings.

422. Louis Untermeyer (1885–1977), American poet and anthologist, a friend of Mencken and Goodman. Untermeyer's best-selling *Modern American Poetry* went into many editions.

423. One can only guess how welcome this committee of busybodies will be!

424. *Allgemeinesgreisenheim:* General Old Folks' Home.

425. *Kartoffelsalat:* Potato salad.

of it in her time. No set-out of the Onkel Braesig Verein[426] was complete without it.

Mencken

Dear Mencken:

In confidence: Elsa Schrakampf, whose mother used to sell horseradish in Lexington Market, is no other than the famous screen star, Mabel Normand.[427] Which explains her facility in registering tears. The old lady left over $20,000 when she died, not counting three properties in Canton Street.[428] It turns out that Strohmeyer, the butter and egg man, never charged her a cent of rent for her little stall. He was a fine fellow through and through and no one felt sorrier than I when he got in that oleo trouble six or seven years ago. I understand that he died penniless. In fact, I know that he had little or nothing after the trial, otherwise he would never have taken a job with George Stockberger, formerly his biggest competitor.

Stockberger, I learn, has grown rich. He just completed a

426. Onkel Braesig Verein: The club is named for a character in Fritz Reuter's *Ut mine Stromtid*, a novel of farm life told in the Low German dialect.

427. Lexington Market, among Baltimore markets, was the largest. Many families went out of their way to go there on Tuesdays and Fridays to visit the best butchers. Mabel Normand (1894–1930) was the vivacious brunette who impressed many as the most talented of America's silent screen comediennes. Her career lasted into the early twenties. She was married to Lew Cody, who made a series of romantic comedies with Aileen Pringle. As for La Pringle, well . . .

428. Canton Street is in the business district of Baltimore, near the waterfront.

house that cost over $100,000 and you couldn't touch his paintings for $75,000. You knew, of course, that he has three Innesses and a Moran.[429] The signatures are plainly inscribed on each of them, so there is no doubt about them. Otto Minzeheimer, the critic, wanted to catalogue his pictures for seventy-five dollars, but Stockberger couldn't see so much money for fully three weeks work. They finally compromised on twenty dollars. To be paid in advance. That was over two years ago. The catalogue never appeared. Minzeheimer promises to get around to it some day.

Goodman

June 20th [1920]

Dear Goodman:

What you observe is simply the pathetic collapse of one of old Grandma Babette Hochschild's well-known plots. I saw the whites of her eyes and got away in time. Granddaughter Celeste is now spending the summer at Blue Ridge Summit,[430] cured, I hope, of her lust for *goyim*. My engagement to Miss Elsa Gundelschläger stands, and will stand. She is a sweet girl, and will come into $30,000 when her mother passes away. I

429. George Inness (1825–94), landscape painter, was one of the most talented members of the Hudson River School. In later years his atmospheric studies placed him in the Impressionist movement. Thomas Moran (1837–1926), landscape painter, was best known for his paintings of western U.S. scenery, especially the Yellowstone region. Goodman loves to deal with human foibles and gullibility, hence his assertion, "there is no doubt," in the following sentence.

430. Blue Ridge Summit, Pennsylvania, is on the Maryland line, south of Chambersburg.

say nothing against the Feinbergs of Hazleton,[431] but before I'd take on such a cousin as Irving Weitzenkorn of Wilkes-Barre I'd go to work. No doubt you have heard that the Circuit Court there has refused him permission to change his name to Wheatly.[432]

Gerhardt Huber, of Frederick, Md., has printed a card in the Frederick *Mail* certifying that Hoover is his cousin—a son of his uncle, Eberhardt J. Huber, of Kienzelsville, in Washington County, Pa.[433] The news has caused a considerable lifting of eyebrows locally.

The younger Hertz boy, Israel, has just married Gladys Hocheimer. It was dam' near time. She can hardly walk.

Mencken

FINIS

431. Hazleton is a town twenty miles south of Wilkes-Barre, Pennsylvania.

432. Wheatly: *Weitzenkorn* translates into "wheat."

433. Herbert Clark Hoover (1874–1964) came to national attention during World War I as administrator of food production, and by 1920 was already being mentioned as a candidate for president. Huber was the original form of the family name, but Gerhardt Huber's spurious claim to being Hoover's cousin is merely the final example in these letters of human pretension.

AFTERWORD

PHILIP GOODMAN, WRITING THE FINAL CHAPTERS OF *Franklin Street* at the time of his death,[1] had not been able to continue his early success. His hit plays were succeeded by flops that used up all his money. An example was the musical *Rainbow*, which his friend James M. Cain, the writer, had warned him was out of his area of expertise, the Broadway comedy. "The play was a complete failure, and on the day of the crash in 1929, Goodman took what little money he had left, said to his daughter Ruth, 'Let's get out of this,' and together they boarded an inexpensive liner for Europe."[2]

When Goodman came back to New York, he produced only one more play, *Washington Heights*, a crushing failure. Thus Goodman, the man who produced the longest-running play on Broadway of his era (*The Old Soak*), who made W. C. Fields a

1. *Franklin Street* was finished after Goodman's death by his daughter, Ruth Goodman Goetz. See *Menckeniana* (Enoch Pratt Free Library) (Winter 1988): 1.

2. Roy Hoopes, *Cain* (New York: Holt, Rinehart, and Winston, 1982), 194.

comedian, who paired his young friend Howard Dietz with the great composer Jerome Kern, who persuaded James M. Cain to write his first play—this Broadway mogul—could find no way to repair his own fortune.

Goodman continued in the 1930s to visit Europe, and what he saw there worried him. A closeup look at the Nazis in Germany made him an anti-Nazi activist and indirectly exacerbated a rift with Mencken that had been growing for years. Mencken, in his letters, tried to soothe Goodman, likening the Nazis to the Ku Klux Klan, predicting that the German people were too smart to be fooled for long. Goodman was incredulous that Mencken could be so blind, not to say seemingly indifferent to the plight of the Jews in the path of the Holocaust. For Mencken's part, he chafed at Goodman's broad-brush condemnation of the Germans and was upset with Goodman for supporting communism as an antidote to fascism.

As Mencken and Goodman's friendship was strained there was also less opportunity to keep it alive. In 1933 Mencken gave up the editorship of the *American Mercury*, and trips to New York were less necessary. Mencken, now married to Sara Powell Haardt, and Goodman, often traveling in Europe or working in Hollywood, did not need the beery evenings and rowdy companionship that had fueled their friendship.

The decline in Goodman's fortunes, and Mencken's eclipse as an editor, were no less factors in their fading bonhomie: in harsher circumstances the old joy was just not there. Their long and spirited correspondence tapered off after 1933, and their friendship was in limbo when Goodman died in 1940. The letters that waited so long to become a book remain to remind us of their great friendship.

ACKNOWLEDGMENTS

BEGINNING TO WRITE ABOUT MENCKEN BRINGS ONE INTO contact with a marvelous community of scholars. Merely to glance at a bookshelf in the home of a Mencken aficionado is to see the wealth of biographical and critical material that this community is publishing, still, forty years after the death of the Sage. This outpouring of books and articles is our way, the scholars' way, of expressing our appreciation of the incomparable man with the great heart who lived at 1524 Hollins Street and still in these later days cheers us like no other writer.

The legacy of Mencken is guarded by Averil J. Kadis and the trustees for the estate of H. L. Mencken at the Enoch Pratt Free Library in Baltimore. It has been an honor to work with them and the many dedicated people at the Pratt who are essential to research. I thank especially Neil R. Jordahl for his early encouragement of this book and Vincent Fitzpatrick, curator of the Mencken Room, for always being there with his vast knowledge of Mencken and the Pratt collection. It was a pleasure to work with John Sondheim and the Pratt's other experts in the humanities. The Pratt is a tremendous resource for any researcher.

The legacy of Goodman has been continued in the work of his daughter Ruth Goodman Goetz and her daughter Judy Sanger. I had the good fortune to visit with Ruth Goetz in her New York home and discuss her father and his friendship with Mencken, as well as her own career in the theater. She gave permission for the letters of Phil Goodman to appear in this book in order to bring her father's special sensibility to a wider audience, and she allowed me to use the evocative photographs of Phil Goodman from the family archives. For a generation she has shared with the Mencken community her great knowledge of the people and the era.

To study Mencken is to be a member of an extended family, and we tend to consult each other regularly. Since we enjoy what we are doing, each opportunity to look into a problem is a new chance to delve into a congenial field of study. I most often took my problems to George H. Thompson, Marion Elizabeth Rodgers, and Professor Richard J. Schrader. George Thompson is a scholar's collector, not only the greatest collector of Mencken material, but someone who has approached the problem of a complete collection with a scholar's eye. He not only knows of any obscure publication but has a copy of it. Marion Rodgers is any Mencken lover's model of editorial style, as seen in her published books, and is currently, as she completes her biography of Mencken, the prime authority on less well-known sides of the Sage's life. Dick Schrader is a genius in the field of bibliography, who not incidentally is compiling the first great work of Mencken bibliography since Betty Adler's, a book that will far surpass the resources that have heretofore been available to readers and scholars.

Charles Wallen Jr., epistolarian without peer, gave me two copies of Philip Goodman's magnum opus, *Franklin Street*, and more than two dozen of the books that I used for research on this project. He is also a source of information about the literature of the twentieth century, of which he is a dedicated reader. He brings an unflagging enthusiasm to the study of Mencken and his age. Professor Frederick Betz, with a deep knowledge of literature, particularly as it pertains to Germany, is another friend, and a useful person to know when you are pursuing an obscure fact. For help with medical allusions—of which Mencken was particularly fond—I turned to my old friend Dr. David M. Priver, who clarified Mencken's abstruse references to the human reproductive system.

I needed to consult frequently with people who knew Baltimore, and Arthur Gutman, president of the Mencken Society, knows Baltimore, Mencken, and the Jewish community. Arthur has been a continuing inspiration of my projects, and a font of information. Randall Bierne has made a study of American immigrants, among his many historical interests, and guided me toward a deeper understanding of the immigrants who came into Baltimore. Mayo DuBasky brought me, from her career at the Library of Congress, an intuitive understanding of the Mencken era of Baltimore, and of Mencken, her special interest. I learned about Baltimore, medicine, and many other things, from Professors Lanny and Dorothy Herron, whose offer of a place to stay within walking distance of the Pratt Library was not the least important assistance I received on this project.

In handling the thorny problems of the German language

presented by the text I was cheerily helped by a teacher in the field, Merriam M. Moore. She read the manuscript with a critical eye, and, as an expert in the field of German genealogical research, helped with German family names. I also consulted the masterly books of Hans Bahlow and George F. Jones.

I would like to thank two essential sources of general support. First my editor, Ernest Scott of the Maryland Historical Society, who brings a lifelong dedication to small-press books to the publications of the Society. He guided the realization of this book. Finally, I thank my wife Carol, who after writing and publishing her own books for two decades is a matchless source of editorial judgment. She patiently reads and critiques every word, and I would not be so foolish as to begin a project like this without assurance of her help.

ABOUT THE EDITOR

JACK SANDERS LIVES AND WORKS IN SAN DIEGO, CALIFORNIA. BY
training he is a lawyer, by occupation a manager of real estate, by incli-
nation a scholar.

Sanders is a humanist, libertarian, skeptic, and curmudgeon. The scion
of a family of robust German peasants, he nevertheless acquired the
trappings of a pedant, and you could drop him into any Heidelberg café
and he would find perfect camouflage among the assembled anarchists.

He inherits from his German roots many traditional views. He has
never said no to a sausage, beer seems to him a more useful beverage
than liquor, and it is said that he reveres every portion of the pig. Men-
tally he remains as sentimental as any Bavarian immigrant, but his
schmaltzy side is tempered by an obsessive urge to completeness, and
he will allow that there is a little of the Prussian in the family tree.

Sanders began work on *Do You Remember?* after reading Philip
Goodman's story of a Philadelphia childhood, *Franklin Street.* He decided that he must read the remaining work of this great observer of
human character. He is delighted to have been able to edit this volume,
which is Goodman's *second* book and Mencken's most outrageous book
of letters.